Community at the Crossroads:

The History of Bayview on Whidbey Island

by Frances L. Wood

The Goosefoot Community Fund
Langley, WA 98260

Community at the Crossroads:
The History of Bayview on Whidbey Island
by Frances L. Wood

No part of this book may be reproduced or transmitted in any form or by any means, electronic or mechanical, including photocopying, recording or by any information storage-and-retrieval system, without written permission from the publisher. Brief passages may be quoted for reviews.

Copyright © 2002 by The Goosefoot Community Fund
All rights reserved.
First printing 2002
Printed in the United States of America

ISBN: 0-9724459-0-0

Published by:
    The Goosefoot Community Fund
    P.O. Box 114
    Langley, WA 98260

To order this book contact:
    Bayview Arts
    P.O. Box 114
    5603 S. Bayview Road
    Langley, WA 98260

    360-321-8414
    e-mail: bayviewarts@whidbey.com

Art direction: Christopher Baldwin
Cover and book design: Sandy Welch
Copy editing and proofing: Marian Blue
Specialized maps: Flat Rock Productions

Cover photos:
    Front: Clockwise from upper right: Betty Schmidt Johnston in front of the Cash Store, Bayview School, Walter (Jack) Jewett with his team, the Burk Brothers' Mill at Lone Lake.

    Back: Delivery truck for original Cash Store located at the Bayview wharf.

*To the many travelers to Bayview,
both those in the past and those yet to come.*

—F.L.W.

Acknowledgements

I wish to acknowledge and thank the many people who assisted with the completion of this book. Only a few are named here; many more were involved and their help was invaluable to me and to recording this history.

First I thank Nancy Nordhoff and Linda Moore of the Goosefoot Community Fund for envisioning this project and supporting its unfolding. Also, I'm grateful to Mary Ann Mansfield and Debbie Torget who provided invaluable assistance whenever asked.

Next, I thank the Bayview Community members who offered their time, memories and photos. Ron Johnston and Judy Johnston Thorsen, Eva Mae and Raymond Gabelein, Jan Kohlwes Witsoe and Arlene Kohlwes Alschbauch-Scott, Lucille Thompson Nourse and Mabel Olsen Alexander participated as guests in "Bayview Live: Stories as Told by our Seniors," community gatherings that grew into radio programs. Sue Frause contributed wit and wisdom to these programs, and I offer her huge thanks.

Other community members who allowed me to interview and collect their stories are Art and Dorothy Burke, Harry and Nora Josephson, Robert and Karen Kohlwes, Mae Stone Kohlwes, Evelyn Hagstrom Varon, Maxine Sanders, Marion Henny and Leda Baker. Many others contributed, including Fran Johnson, Norma Metcalf, Jonni Reed and Duke LeBaron. I particularly acknowledge the help of Winnie McLeod and the South Whidbey Historical Society.

Personally, I thank my husband Bill Graves. And especially Colleen Bollen, Paul Freeman, Julie Jindal, Indu Sundaresan and Phil Winberry for their insight and support.

Contents

Community at the Crossroads:
The History of Bayview on Whidbey Island

Chapter 1	Discovering Bayview Today......................	1
Chapter 2	Before European Settlement....................	9
Chapter 3	The Europeans Arrive..............................	19
Chapter 4	A Community Called "Bay View"...........	31
Chapter 5	Bayview Becomes a Corner....................	43
Chapter 6	Bayview Corner Grows............................	63
Chapter 7	Bayview Corner Revived..........................	83

Chronology of Early Bayview........................... 93

Resources... 97
Photo Credits... 100
Index... 101

Discovering Bayview Today

Disembarking from a Washington State Ferry at the Clinton dock, I fall in line with a string of cars heading north up Whidbey Island. Leaving Clinton, SR 525 relaxes into the quiet rolling hills of South Whidbey, skirts the strip mall at Ken's Korner, passes an old cranberry bog, and approaches Casey's Market. On this clear and sunny day, the Olympic Mountains in their deep blue and icy white brilliance appear over the trees to the west. The road begins an almost imperceptible decline into a swale, and the Douglas fir, hemlock and cedar give way to lowland alder and willow.

Chapter 1: Bayview Corner Today

Shortly past Casey's Market, the highway intersects Bayview Road. Since the completion of a bypass in the late 1950s, it's easy to miss Bayview Corner—three large, historic buildings set beyond a mowed field. Most people driving up the highway wouldn't know that the former Cash Store building now houses a busy restaurant, community meeting room and office space. Or that Bayview Hall, built in 1928, still hosts Saturday night dances. Or that the historic Bayview School after periods of disuse once again rings with students' voices.

Whizzing past the corner, an oversized American flag above the Whidbey Telephone Company calls for attention. Just beyond the phone company buildings, the road reaches a low point in the valley and bends to the left. Here a wide vista opens across a 600-acre field of flat farmland that extends to the distant southern horizon. Along the field's edge I spot a northern harrier, a marsh-nesting hawk, glide moth-like over the tangles of blackberry mounds hiding a meandering slough. This slough, quietly flowing through a culvert under the highway, is the outfall from Lone Lake a half mile to the north. From here the highway begins to climb and continues up Whidbey Island. It passes by Freeland, Greenbank, Coupeville and Oak Harbor. Finally, forty miles north of the Clinton ferry dock, the highway exits the island via the Deception Pass Bridge.

Back at the intersection with Bayview Road, I could make a different decision. Instead of driving past, I pull out of the fast lane toward the slower pace of the crossroads called Bayview Corner. I turn to the right off the highway, like every vehicle going up island before the bypass was built.

On this sunny Saturday in the summer of 2002, I follow signs toward the Farmers' Market and soon turn left into a grassy field to park. Curiously, the ground, though green and grassy, feels solid. Walking past Bayview Hall, I'm attracted to the busy Market, a group of stalls under a tall spreading maple tree. Wandering among the fifty or so vendors, I inspect fresh locally grown vegetables, home baked desserts, hand-crafted chairs, lavender sachets and a simple bouquet of cobalt blue iris. A display from the Beach Watchers, a local environmental organization, offers information about fresh water conservation for this island, which depends on underground aquifers for its annual recharge. At another table, a woman sells raffle tickets to help preserve a beautiful second growth forest located nearby. Friendly chatter circles through groups of locals and visitors—the weather is holding, the beans are just coming in and did you happen to catch the local band, *No Band is an Island*, last night at Bayview Hall?

The smell of fresh coffee—organic, fair-traded and shade grown—draws me to the old Cash Store, a wooden two-story

Visitors to Bayviews Farmers' Market can select locally grown organic vegetables, flowers, crafts, hand-made clothing and home baked goods. The outdoor market is open on Saturdays from spring to fall.

Chapter 1: Bayview Corner Today

structure of jumbled add-ons. Through a white picket fence and past flowerbeds of old-fashioned roses, I enter a warm, cozy eatery, The Smilin' Dog. After a huge homemade cookie and a double tall cappuccino, I step deeper into the 1920s building to discover a large meeting room open for whatever community event beckons—church suppers, a display of Peruvian handicrafts or an Open Mic featuring bluegrass music. For a mere five dollars and a promise to clean and lock up, a group can rent this room, which holds one hundred people.

In 1993 Maureen and Jim Rowley established Bayview Farm and Garden. The business sells an extensive offering of plants as well as garden and farm supplies.

Exiting out a side door, I saunter through an outdoor sculpture garden and pause to watch a large granite cone gurgling with water as it rotates on a 2,500-pound base. Turning back toward the market I notice a wisteria-canopied archway beckoning toward a nursery, Bayview Farm and Garden, with brightly colored flowers, greenhouses and acres of outdoor plants.

Built by the Bayview community in 1928, Bayview Hall still holds dances, performances, parties and anniversary celebrations.

I resist the nursery and wander into Bayview Arts housed in an old revamped garage. Art supplies delightfully mingle with locally made crafts, like candy for the eyes. Next I stroll back toward Bayview Hall, a large, white, rectangular building with a new sky-blue metal roof and turquoise trim. Famous for its fine wood dance floor, the community-owned building hosts a flea market this particular summer day. I browse through used books, clothing, polished stones, buttons, tools and odds and ends that can be purchased for bargain prices.

Stepping out the side door, I notice an odd-shaped structure tucked behind the hall. A sharply peaked roof floats on a wide veranda porch roof. The walls, which look both modern and earthy, are part metal and part wooden branches set in concrete. A nearby kiosk explains that this, the public restroom for Bayview Corner, is a high-tech composting toilet, a demonstration of sustainable design. The metal panels of the kiosk are recycled colored aluminum from the Experience Music Project in Seattle. I begin to sense a

Chapter 1: Bayview Corner Today

A unique, new addition to Bayview Corner is the high-tech composting toilet. This serves as the public restrooms for the Corner.

new purpose at Bayview Corner. More than just a jumble of old buildings or the happenstance of funky charm, Bayview Corner is a huge recycle project.

The Goosefoot Community Fund, the Corner's owner since 1999, has created a model of what it envisions a community should be: a lively gathering place hosting a multi-faceted range of activities and preserving valued links to the past. The kiosk calls it *"a national model of rural planning, practical environmentalism, skillful investment and community imagination."*

The comfort-food-goodness and blend of art and nostalgia seem like a wonderful coincidence, one of those miracles of non-planning that produces a place that just feels right. But this is no accident. The folks at Goosefoot intentionally set out to make us feel, deep in our bones, that we've come home to a very comfortable, welcoming spot.

The kiosk also explains how Bayview Corner is a model for integrating sustainable design concepts. The open grassy field where I parked is reinforced with Geoblock, a low impact system to support vehicles but allow rainwater infiltration. This accounts for the firmness of the grass I noticed when first arriving. The storm water pond required by the county at the Bayview Road intersection will offer wildlife habitat as well as control for storm run off. Rain barrels and on-site composting top a long list of future plans.

Sitting on a bench under an old gnarled apple tree I wonder how this 120-year-old community gathering place evolved and how it has been sustained into the 21st century. How

Near the restroom another modern structure, The Kiosk, explains the mission and programs of the Goosefoot Community Fund. Notices of events are posted as well as explanations of the sustainable design concepts used at the corner.

Chapter 1: Bayview Corner Today

has the Goosefoot Community Fund been able to blend the old and the new so gracefully? Certainly it was good fortune to find an historic area that has not changed much over the years. But the answer is more complex than that. To help answer that question we need to look back in time to the beginnings of Bayview Corner.

Flower vendors add colorful charm to a Saturday stroll through the Farmers' Market.

In the 1850s homesteaders, who had the whole island to choose from, decided to stake their claim here. Using meager resources—physical strength, determination and a dream—early settlers looked at the bay, the fresh water from Lone Lake, the massive stands of old-growth forest, the abundant game and fish, and said, "Yep, this is it!"

But Bayview's history really begins even before that.

Chapter 2

Before European Settlement

The Vashon Glacier, the last of several colossal land-shapers, finally left Puget Sound 12,500 years ago as it retreated north into Canada and into the surrounding mountain ranges. Between the Cascades to the east and the Olympics to the west, the glacier left a 100-mile-long trough, the basic landforms we see today. Fresh water from the melting glaciers mixed with salt water flowing from the Pacific Ocean through the Straits of Juan de Fuca and formed a long, multi-fingered, inland sea. The deposits of glacial till above sea level formed a long, snake-like island with its head near what is now the Canadian border and its tail just 30 miles north of present-day Seattle.

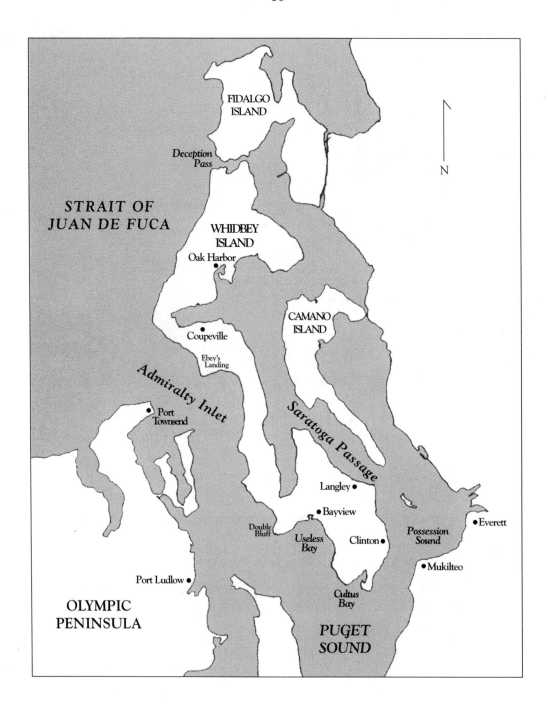

Community at the Crossroads: The History of Bayview on Whidbey Island

The first inhabitants, who arrived soon after the glaciers left, called the island *Illahee,* meaning "the place where we live." Another local tribe called it *Tscha-kole-chy.* Today we call it Whidbey Island. The early people did not divide themselves into named tribes, but to help identify their groupings European settlers have named them by the rivers they called home. The Nisqually, Suquamish and Puyallup peoples lived south of Whidbey Island, the Lummi and Swinomish to the north. The island itself was home to two main groups, the Skagit in the north and the Snohomish to the south. These groups established permanent settlements along the eastern, more protected side of the island opposite their mainland home rivers that flowed down from the Cascade Mountains. Another group, the Klallam, established a toehold on the island's most western bulge. Their dwellings were easily accessed from the Klallam's primary villages across Puget Sound on the Olympic Peninsula and north in the San Juan Islands. Historians classify these groups of native Americans as salt water or canoe people.

Facing page:
Northern Puget Sound showing Whidbey Island and how it settles into the surrounding land forms.

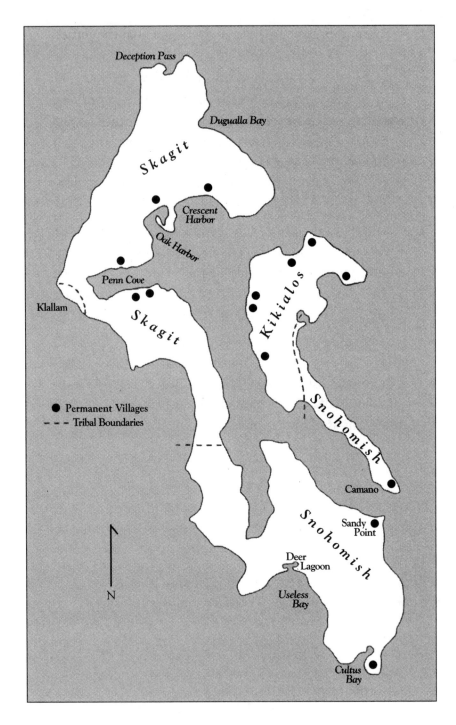

Community at the Crossroads: The History of Bayview on Whidbey Island

The Snohomish maintained a large, permanent settlement of perhaps 100 people eight miles southeast of Bayview Corner at Cultus Bay. Called Digwadsh, the village was an important potlatch center. On calm days these early residents traveled by dugout canoe out of Cultus Bay, west around Scatchet Head, north past what became Maxwelton Beach and into a large shallow bay.

These waters of Useless Bay produced an abundance of crab, clams and fish. Heron waded in the incoming tide, long legs and neck adapted to fishing the shallow waters. Rafts of ducks migrated in during the fall to spend the winter away from the Alaskan cold. Facing south, the sandy beaches surrounding the horseshoe-shaped bay offered warmth by soaking up even the faintest rays of sun. Today, local folks tell me that weather patterns create a hole in the clouds over this bay, even when the rest of South Whidbey is covered in clouds. If true, presumably the early peoples noticed and enjoyed this phenomenon as well, seeking out the warmth of the sandy beaches surrounding the shallow bay.

Facing page:
Prior to European settlement, three Native American tribes lived and fished on Whidbey, the Snohomish to the south, the Skagit in the middle and to the north and the Klallam on the western tip. Permanent villages were scattered around Penn Cove and on the southeastern section of the island.

Chapter 2: Before European Settlement

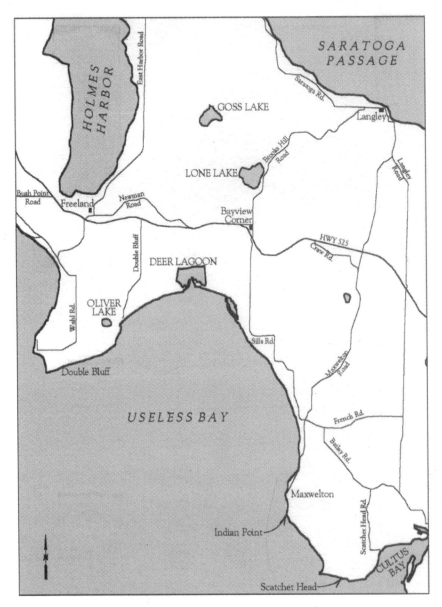

Useless Bay and the surrounding land marks. Present day communities and roads are included for reference.

At the top of the horseshoe, the spot where I would drive in a single nail to hang it on a giant wall, the sandy beach separated and opened into a lagoon, now called Deer Lagoon. This inner sanctum bulged to the east and the west into two marshy halves like a giant pair of eyeglasses. Opposite the entrance to the lagoon sandy cliffs rose abruptly—the nose-bridge of the glasses—topped with old-growth forests that covered the bluff like a deep green quilt.

History suggests, and I can imagine, that during high tide the early peoples paddled through the lagoon's entrance or pulled their dugout canoes up and over the sand spits that framed the entrance. Once inside, they turned east canoeing up the meandering slough between the sandy spit and the cliff, and then bent northeast along the forested hillside continuing up toward the outfall from Lone Lake. They may have lingered on their way at a small temporary village located on the left bank near the site of the present Useless Bay Golf and Country Club. I expect that a pair of bald eagles, early ancestors of present eagle inhabitants, lorded over them from a perch in an old spire of Douglas fir. The eagles would have found easy pickings from the fish that swam through the estuary toward Lone Lake. And the native peoples would have welcomed this symbol of the Great Spirit and searched for eagle feathers under their favorite perching trees.

Chapter 2: Before European Settlement

Over the eons the slough has switched back and forth across the 600-acre estuary to create a wide flat marshland. Along the soft edge between tide and vegetation, deer prints mingled with tracks of red fox, bear and elk. If the paddlers continued north up the outfall, the slough narrowed. Marsh wrens called from the sedge, and swallows cruised the air for gnats and other flying insects. Finally, nearly a half mile from the bay, the bottom of the canoe lagged against the shallow channel, and over-reaching willow branches obstructed the way. A few strong pushes with cedar paddles against the soft bottom brought the canoe to an open patch of muddy shore. Stepping out of the canoe, scrambling up a low bank and looking out to the south, the paddlers had an extraordinary view back toward the bay.

"The deep curve of Useless Bay ends in a lagoon, protected on the west by the long arm of Double Bluff. Prior to 1900, the land around the lagoon was a huge natural park, filled with trees as large as 15 feet in diameter. Fir, hemlock and cedar grew in abundance with ferns, salal and huckleberry at their feet. The waters of the lagoon were navigable at high tide up to within half a mile of the south end of Lone Lake. In places wild grass sprouted between the trees providing food for deer; hence the name Deer Lagoon."[1]

Recently, I stood at this same spot—one half mile from Lone Lake—where Highway 525 now dips at Bayview Corner and looked carefully toward the south. Even with the sun shining brightly and without a cloud in the sky, I couldn't see Useless Bay or what remains of Deer Lagoon. Now the view holds acres of marshy farmland and a far-away row of houses.

Before 1900, the slough extended up to this point and shallow-draft boats managed their way to a wharf. Bayview could claim the status of a port. However, ambitious land reclamation projects dramatically changed the area, transforming 600 acres from estuary to farmland. But I've skipped ahead in our story of Bayview Corner. Let's go back a century to the early visits by European explorers.

---

[1] Lorna Cherry, *South Whidbey and Its People*, *Vol. II, page 127.*

The Europeans Arrive

In 1792 three large sailing vessels entered the blue-gray waters of Puget Sound. Shining like brilliant comets they foretold a century of change. In May of that year, the English explorer Captain George Vancouver sailed his fleet through the Straits of Juan de Fuca, veered south at Protection Island and became the first official European visitor to Whidbey Island. The first documented contact with Whidbey soil occurred on June 2, 1792, when Vancouver came ashore at Penn Cove, an inlet in the north central part of the island.

Chapter 3: The Europeans Arrive

Some historians speculate that the first visit took place three weeks earlier and much closer to Bayview when Vancouver's ships anchored overnight off what is now South Whidbey State Park. Perhaps his crew rowed to shore to collect drinking water.[1] We do know that Vancouver bestowed the name Whidbey's Island in honor of his first lieutenant Joseph Whidbey. During reconnaissance trips Lieutenant Whidbey discovered Deception Pass and proved that Whidbey was an island and not a long peninsula. Various spellings have been used over the years— Whidbey's Island, Whidby Island and Whitby Island—but the official spelling today is Whidbey Island.

> *The country in the vicinity of this branch of the sea is, according to Mr. Whidbey's representation, the finest we have yet met with, notwithstanding the very pleasing appearance of many others; its natural productions were luxuriant in the highest degree, and it was, by no means, ill supplied with streams of fresh water.*
> —from Captain Vancouver's journal

Prior to encountering Vancouver and his crew, Whidbey Island's Indians had no firsthand experience with Europeans. However, Vancouver noted in his journals that abandoned Indian villages and scarred faces suggested the ravages of European-introduced smallpox. He was right. Smallpox had preceded Vancouver to Puget Sound by at least a decade. The disease was brought from the interior by infected Indians, who were exposed to the disease by overland explorers. The white people's diseases spread rapidly throughout the

Puget Sound region and to the Indians of Whidbey Island. In 1780, the Native American population of Whidbey and Camano Islands was between 1,500 and 2,500.[2] Sixty years later, it was half that number. By 1900 the census found only 44 Indians living in Island County.

During the 1830s more explorers and trappers entered the waters around Whidbey Island. In 1840 Father Blanchet, a Catholic missionary from Fort Nisqually, visited the Indians around the Ebey's Prairie area and held services. During his stay a huge wooden cross was erected.

Early launch with sail. At high tide, this type of boat could navigate through the estuary of Deer Lagoon to the wharf at Bayview.

The first non-native to record observations in the Bayview area was Lieutenant Charles Wilkes of the United States Navy, who extensively explored and mapped Whidbey Island in 1841. He named the vast expanse of water between Double Bluff and Indian Point (near Maxwelton) "Useless Bay." The name aptly describes the bay from a sailor's perspective. It lacks shelter against storms and is unfit for larger ships because low tide exposes the shallow sandy bottom. Indians and early settlers found otherwise, enjoying its bounty of crab, clams and fish.

In 1846 the United States and England negotiated a treaty that granted Whidbey Island to the United States. Four

Chapter 3: The Europeans Arrive

years later, Isaac Ebey registered the first claim on Whidbey for prairie land near what we now call Coupeville. Soon after, in 1855, the Indians of Whidbey Island ceded all of Island County to the whites in the Point Elliott Treaty signed in Mukilteo. Many Whidbey Island Indians relocated to the Tulalip reservation north of Everett.

Meanwhile, across Admiralty Inlet on the northeast corner of the Olympic Peninsula, the frontier towns of Port Townsend and Port Ludlow rumbled with activity, spurred mostly by the logging industry. Visitors from Port Townsend regularly hunted and fished the western shores of Whidbey including the Useless Bay and Deer Lagoon areas. The earliest person to leave a permanent record was Edward Oliver, a 20-year-old man from Virginia. Oliver was drawn by tales of the huge trees on South Whidbey where 400- to 600-year-old Douglas fir, hemlock, cedar and white fir sometimes reached a diameter of 15 feet and stood 300 feet tall. South Whidbey's thick, old-growth forests contained some of the largest concentrations of big trees in the world and rivaled the Amazon rainforests.[3] In the late 1850s Oliver boarded the boat *Glencoe* and traveled across Admiralty Inlet through Useless Bay. He landed at the head of Deer Lagoon near what later became Bayview, with the intention to stay.[4]

If the modern image of a Puget Sound logger is big, burly and dark-haired, Oliver was the opposite. He stood just 5 feet 6 inches and weighed only 135 pounds. His small size, blue eyes, light sandy hair and blond flowing beard and mustache made him look more like a minister or teacher than a lumberman.

Despite his diminutive physique, Oliver began logging in the area. I've not been able to discover exactly where he logged or whether he worked by himself or for a logging company. Some reports state that he ran a logging camp for the next ten years, possibly the Stetson-Post Camp, in the area northwest of Deer Lagoon. Other reports specify that he logged near a former Indian encampment, approximately at the location of the present day Useless Bay Golf and Country Club. I've found no record that he purchased land north of Deer Lagoon.

Walter (Jack) Jewett hitched up his team to pull a wagon full of lumber.

After Island County was surveyed, Oliver decided to buy land. In 1874 Oliver purchased 164.40 acres overlooking Sunlight Beach from the Government Land Office for a total of $205.50. Not long after his land purchase, Oliver married Melvinia Sooy who was half Snohomish Indian. The 1880 census recorded Edward as 41 and Melvinia as 20 with a one-year-old daughter named Hester. After three more babies, Melvinia died in 1886.

Now let's back up a few years and briefly trace the history of another early settler, William T. Johnson. The earliest record for Johnson is that he "settled" land on Double

Chapter 3: The Europeans Arrive

Bluff.[5] Johnson had taken a Snohomish Indian wife named Gah-toh-litsa or Jane Newbury. The Double Bluff property probably came to Johnson from Jane's tribe. William and Jane had several children; the oldest, Louisa, was considered the first child born into the white settlement at Useless Bay.

Then in 1886, the same year Melvinia Oliver died, more tragedy hit this small group of settlers.

William Johnson farmed his land and occasionally rowed across Admiralty Inlet to Port Townsend or Port Ludlow to sell his vegetables and other produce. He would head out of Deer Lagoon at high tide and return a day or two later. One such trip occurred on February 27, 1886. The following is Lorna Cherry's account.

Gah-toh-litsa was her Snohomish tribal name, Jane Newbury her English name. She married William T. Johnson and, after his death, married Edward Oliver. Throughout her life she lived at Double Bluff.

"Having transacted his business in Port Townsend where he received a considerable sum of money from the sale of his produce, he embarked on his homeward journey but he never reached home. Instead, he was found dead in his boat the following morning. There was no sign of violence and his death was presumed by the authorities to have been from natural causes, but his family believed differently because no money was found on his person or in the boat, although he

was known to have left Port Townsend with a sizable sum. His family believed that he was murdered for his money."[6]

Foul play or natural causes? I calculated that Johnson was 64 at the time of his death. Port Townsend is 15 miles from Double Bluff across Admiralty Inlet, and it takes today's high-powered ferries nearly an hour to travel that distance. Rowing that far even in calm weather would be strenuous, and February is often stormy. But if natural causes explain the death, what happened to the money? At least for now, this remains an unsolved mystery. One more fact to add to the intrigue: Johnson's widow Jane married the widower Edward Oliver the following year.

This photo looking southeast toward Deer Lagoon, Sunlight Beach and Useless Bay was taken before 1911.

Shortly after, Edward moved from his land above Sunlight Beach and joined Jane at the Double Bluff property where they had six additional children. The property included a large lake, called Oliver Lake, in a swale on the top of the bluff.

There is one additional early settler I must bring into the story. Shortly after Oliver initially came to Bayview back in 1858, he returned to Port Townsend looking for help and

Chapter 3: The Europeans Arrive

found a 17-year-old young man named Thomas Johns. Many years later his arrival on United States soil was recounted in the local newspaper:

"Thomas John Johns joined the English navy at 17 and sailed two years later (1859) from England around the southern tip of South America to Esquimault, B.C., near Victoria. He and eight others in the crew were intrigued with the country and decided to stay.

This meant deserting ship.

All nine got into one of the ship's small white hull boats in the dead of night. They rowed all night and the next day in the overloaded craft, heading south. They landed near Dungeness not far from Port Townsend the next evening. They hid in an old chicken house for the rest of the night. In the morning they decided to separate so they wouldn't be captured and returned home. Johns went to Port Ludlow and bought some denims and discarded his English uniform.

There he met Ed Oliver who suggested a logging partnership with him near Deer Lagoon on Whidbey Island. Thomas agreed and later fell in love with the Island."[7]

I expect the backwater of Bayview seemed a safe haven for this illegal immigrant. For the next decade Johns and Oliver logged in the area. In 1872 Thomas Johns filed an intent to purchase land on the east side of Deer Lagoon. Soon after, on April 12, 1874, he married a woman named Mary Jane Coffelt, and they had three children, the oldest a daughter named Florence. Strangley, I found no record of a Thomas Johns or his family in the 1880 census although there is little doubt that he was residing in Bayview. However, there is a record of a

Thomas Johnson, an Englishman with a wife named Mary and a one-year-old daughter named Florence. This seems an unlikely coincidence, and I expect that Thomas Johns didn't want his whereabouts officially recorded. Johns remained a very active community member for over three decades, using the name Thomas Johns.

Taken prior to 1911, this photo looks west from the area of Sunlight Beach Road. Sunlight Beach spit is on the right. In the middle is the old Blankenberg lumber mill.

During the 1870s and 1880s, lumbering was a major contributor to the Island County economy. Three logging camps existed on South Whidbey, one at Bayview. At first, logs were hauled to saltwater beaches and towed by tugs across the sound to be milled in Port Townsend and Port Ludlow.

Later a mill was built on the east side of Useless Bay. Robert Kohlwes, grandson of William and Mary Kohlwes remembered this old mill, called the Blankenberg Mill. *"The old mill was quite a large mill. It was steam operated and had a governor to regulate the power. As the logs went through, the noise coming from the mill changed. That was a nostalgic sound I remember from my childhood. Old Paul Blankenberg was a quiet guy, a kind of a character who lived in a long, low house next to*

Chapter 3: The Europeans Arrive

Looking north past Indian Point toward Sunlight Beach. Photo taken in 1887.

the mill. He fixed old stoves and was always working on something. He liked to eat Limburger cheese, too." As logging moved inland and hauling trees to the water became more difficult, a sawmill was built on Lone Lake.

> **THE LONE LAKE MILL**
>
> About 1910 this sawmill, the Lone Lake Mill Company, was owned and operated by my Dad, John D. Burk, his brother, William and an uncle Barney Boch. The woods in the background provided the timber logged and cut into lumber which was hauled to Langley by horse and wagon. Early settlers like Jacob Anthes, purchased the lumber to build their homes in Langley.
>
> The house on the left in the picture was the boarding house for the mill hands. Later my parents moved there and that was where I was born. The house on the right was my Uncle Will's and his family. One of my cousins was Charles Burk who owned the Langley Lumber Company until recently when he retired. Chuck started the second grade at Bayview School about the time this picture was taken.
>
> Several years later the mill burned. The two Burk brothers built the Maple Leaf Mill at Midvale. From the lumber he cut at his own mill, my Uncle Will built the Bayview Cash store. He later sold the store to Harold Johnston who owned it for many years.
>
> After the new mill was finished, the house by the Bayview Road was torn down. My father, John Burk, then built a Shell Gasoline Station there. He also used some of the other small buildings to make a fishing resort which he ran for years on Lone Lake.
>
> This mill site was located just South of the present Deer Lagoon Grange. I have recently built a cabin where the old house was and Attorney John Watson's place is on the old sawdust pile.
>
> Arthur J. Burk

Description of Lone Lake Mill and the Burk family businesses.

The Burk Brothers' mill on Lone Lake. The mill burned in 1914.

Walter Seiforth, who lived in the same house near Bayview for over 70 years, described the logging business. *"They would cut down trees three and four feet in diameter with two man-made saws and spring-boards–which were flat pieces of iron and a two-by-six that they put in a notch in a tree and would [climb up on to saw through the tree above the splayed trunk]. Cutting the trees was a back-breaking job. Eight trees in one day was considered a good day's work... After the trees were cut, the men would put them on skids and oxen would haul them to the beach. Then they would float the logs to a small saw mill that used to be at Bayview."*[8]

Today springboard stumps can still be seen mixed in among the second- and third-growth trees in forested areas around Bayview.

---

[1] The South Whidbey Record, November 16, 1978

[2] Richard White, *Land Use, Environment, and Social Change: The Shaping of Island County Washington*, page 15.

Chapter 3: The Europeans Arrive

[3] Richard White, *Land Use, Environment, and Social Change: The Shaping of Island County Washington*, page 78.

[4] Lorna Cherry in her book, *South Whidbey and Its People* states that Oliver arrived in Bayview in 1858. She also reports that Oliver was 28 at the time. However, Oliver was born in 1839, which puts his age closer to 20 if we assume that Oliver arrived in 1859.

[5] Spindrift Magazine, Summer 1998. Later in 1873, Johnson purchased this piece, 153.65 acres, for $192.

[6] Lorna Cherry, *South Whidbey and Its People*, Vol. I page 61.

[7] The South Whidbey Record, June 10, 1976.

[8] Lorna Cherry, *South Whidbey and Its People*, Vol. II, page 146.

A Community Called "Bay View"

It is hard to say when a scattering of loggers and a few families become a community. Perhaps it happens when an area takes on a name or when folks decide to build a community hall. Perhaps it happens when a school is organized or a church is formed. If those assumptions are correct, I would suggest that the Bayview community began to coalesce in the 1880s. The name Bayview was first written as Bay View. One source credits Thomas Johns' wife Mary with naming the community.[1] The name Bay View was in common use by 1886.

Early Bayview Community Hall. Photo taken about 1900.

A community hall— a simple, one-room log structure — had been built around 1880. Located about 100 yards south of the present Bayview School, the early building housed community events, church services, basket socials, Sunday school and possibly the early school. Local resident Mabel Alexander described the building, *"I remember vaguely there was an old building on the school grounds. My mom used to play a guitar there, and they danced, and held plays."*[2] Others have reported a large wood stove burned in a corner to stave off the winter cold and dampness.

Before there was a school in Bayview, students traveled by horseback through the woods to a school near Sandy Point, southeast of Langley. In 1886 a school opened in Bayview and records exist from the first year. According to the School District Clerk's Annual Report, early settler Thomas Johns (using the name Johns, not Johnson) was the first clerk of the school, a position he held for at least three decades. W. Luther Weedin, who owned land near the outfall of Lone Lake, served as director of the school. In 1886 three of the eight students enrolled in the school were Johns' children: the daughter Florence, now seven years old; and twin sons Willie and James, who both drowned when they were 19.[3] Another student was Edward Oliver's youngest child, Eddie. Two Peterson and two Weedin offspring completed the first class. The school term lasted three months, and the teacher was paid $40 per month. The estimated value of school furnishings was $16. Twenty-two children of school age living in the Bayview area chose not to attend school that first year.

According to the report, the school had neither a dictionary nor a building. Stories differ as to where the school met. Some recollect that classes were held in a converted cookhouse on the Herbert Weedin farm, located next to Deer Lagoon marsh.[4] It is also reported that the old log building south of the present school was used for classes around the turn of the twentieth century. Perhaps both are true.

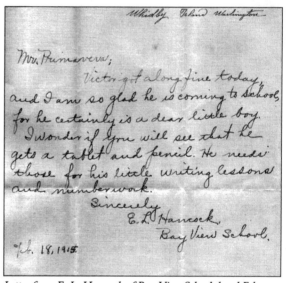

Letter from E. L. Hancock of Bay View School dated February 18, 1915.

A decade later the enrollment had increased to 18 students, but the teacher's salary had dropped to $35. The 1896 records show that *"School closed September 18-25 for the [Island County] Fair."* Later in the year it also closed *"for two weeks,*

Chapter 4: A Community Called "Bay View"

account of chicken-pox." Around 1900 the school acquired a Webster's Unabridged Dictionary. Amazingly, as I paged through the official school record book for that year, I discovered a handful of pressed four-leaf clovers–frail but still tinted green. I can picture young Johns, Weedin, Olson and Thompson pupils searching the school yard for the four-leafed clovers and presenting the bouquet to their teacher, Ethel Sanford.

Bayview School soon after it opened in 1909. The bell tower was later removed and very recently the bell was re-hung in a structure in front.

After 1900, school attendance expanded rapidly, and around 1909 a proper wooden school building was built.[5] George Bump donated land for the school on the hill just above Bayview Road. The large structure consisted of two wings, and a belfry topped the roof. One building wing housed the first four grades, the other housed the upper four. Two teachers were hired. *"Each room had a large wood stove that stood on legs and was six feet high with a shield around it. The boys took turns bringing in wood for the stove. There were 'his' and 'her' outhouses back of the school."*[6]

By 1910, 71 students attended Bayview School. The school equipment list for that year shows 23 erasers, 75 tablets, 12 pencils, seven dictionaries, one waterbucket, one wash basin, two teacher's desks and an Eight Day Clock. Also included is the title of each of the 148 books in the school library. Most were well-known classics such as *Ivanhoe, Little Lord Fauntleroy, Great Expectations, Oliver Twist, Gulliver's*

Travels, Black Beauty and *Ben Hur*. Also on the list were *Ettiquette* [sic], *First Principles of Agriculture, Christmas Stories* and *The Tale of Bunny Cotton Tail*. Despite a new, well-equipped school building and a relatively large library, none of the 8th grade students passed the county exams that year.[7] However, a baseball diamond filled up the play yard, and the team excelled against other Whidbey Island teams.

Bayview Cemetery. The original land for this cemetery was donated by Thomas Johns and William Weedin in 1905.

Perhaps another characteristic to identify when a haphazard group of people becomes a community is when they establish a cemetery. Prior to 1905 deceased family members were buried on the family land. As the population of Bayview grew and sections of land were broken into smaller pieces, the community needed to designate an area for burying the dead. A site was chosen on top of the hill on the east side of Deer Lagoon along Bayview Road. The land was owned by Thomas Johns and William Weedin who each donated one acre for the cemetery. The deed for the cemetery property indicated that the Weedin family and the Johns family would each retain ownership of one plot in the cemetery.

Chapter 4: A Community Called "Bay View"

Gravestones for members of the Johns and Weedin families are still visible in the old sections of the cemetery.

The Bayview Cemetery Association formed and elected R. H. Millman as president, F. A. Harth as secretary and J. G. Melendy as trustee. Work began to clear and fence one acre of the land on September 18, 1905. A year later at the annual business meeting of the association, the trustees set the price for a cleared plot, $10 or four days of work. Evidently, even the work option didn't compel family members to pay. A few years later in 1909 the trustees became more assertive. They voted to remove bodies from the cemetery if the fee wasn't paid within one year. These bodies were reburied in a field, called Potter's field.

During the next two decades familiar names such as William Kohlwes and Henry Tiemeyer served as trustees of the cemetery association. In 1925 the association voted to plant trees along the road at the front of the cemetery. An upkeep fee of $1 per year for each plot was levied and the group decided on an annual workday to spruce up the grounds.

After nearly half a century the community needed more land for its cemetery. In 1950, 15 more acres across Bayview Road were added to the cemetery property. Several years later in 1984 the community decided that the new cemetery needed more trees. At a tree-planting party, 47 flowering trees were planted. But I've jumped ahead in the story. Let's return to the beginning of the twentieth century and take a look at the industry that replaced timber and brought even more settlers to Bayview: farming.

Harvesting timber from around Deer Lagoon and Lone Lake opened the land for farming. According to *Island County a World Beater*, a promotional piece written in 1911, there were *"a large number of prosperous farms overlooking the beautiful waters of Useless Bay."*[8] Several German families including the Tiemeyers, Schumachers, Ackermans, Meyers, Gabeleins and Kohlweses settled in the area. Letters back to family and friends in Germany and other parts of the United States spread the word of opportunities in the Bayview area. The community formed a German Lutheran church, hired a pastor and built a church on Lone Lake.

Home of Mr. C. E. Ackerman about 1910, looking west. Mr. Ackerman owned 15 acres where he had dairy cows, poultry and grew fruit and vegetables. Ackerman encouraged families from Germany to settle in the Bayview area.

Home of Mrs. Louisa Tiemeyer about 1910. Mrs. Tiemeyer successfully grew wheat, oats vetch and hogs on her 80-acre farm.

Chapter 4: A Community Called "Bay View"

Oliver sold his 164 acres to the east of Deer Lagoon to William Tiemeyer in 1886, twelve years after he bought it from the Government Land Office for $205.50. This time the land sold for $1,000. Later in 1902, Tiemeyer sold it to William and Mary Kohlwes for $4,000. Mary Kohlwes, originally Mary Thuvesson, came from Sweden and represented another group of European immigrants. Her name Thuvesson was Anglicized to Thompson.

Farm of William and Mary Kohlwes about 1910. The Kohlweses owned 98 acres at this time where they cultivated wheat, oats, potatoes and carrots and raised hogs, dairy and poultry.

William and Mary Kohlwes with their oldest son Frederick, about 1902. Frederick was the first white child born above the Arctic Circle in the Territory of Alaska. When he was one year-old the family moved to Bayview.

From the late 1890s through 1915 the hub of Bayview activity was the small wharf at the outfall of Lone Lake. Shallow-draft boats traveled into Useless Bay and up the slough to discharge and receive people and merchandise at the wharf. A 1914 map shows a dock, landing and *"about 3.0 feet water at high tide"*[9] next to the Luther Weedin property. A small warehouse on the shore was equipped with a loading

Community at the Crossroads: The History of Bayview on Whidbey Island

dock for taking goods off the boats. North of the dock and warehouse stood the first Bayview Cash Store built and owned by Adolph Meier (also referred to as Ernie Meyers). The store, which stocked basic groceries for settlers and feed and grain for their animals, was built about 1908.

The old Bayview Cash Store located just up from the wharf. Photo taken about 1910.

The 1914 map also shows a small dock next to the Cram property, which was located south of the Weedin land. Fred Kohlwes, son of William and Mary Kohlwes, remembers a boat named *Sedro* that belonged to Bernie Cram. *"It would come into Useless Bay on a high tide with supplies for the Bayview Store. After he had delivered the supplies, Bernie would have to stay over until the next high tide before he could take the boat out of the bay."* [10]

Home of Adolph Meier taken about 1910. At this time he owned the original Bayview Cash Store and supplied the community with general merchandise.

An early Bayview post office was located at the Melendy farm.

Bernie Cram also brought the mail into Bayview by boat. An early post office operated out of the Melendy home and at other times from the Bayview Cash Store. Sometime before 1911, the mail began to arrive by land from Langley. *"Walter Hunziker was the mail carrier and he recalls riding out to Bayview on horseback to deliver and pick up the mail."* [11]

Realizing the limitation of the high tide wharf at Bayview, settlers improved the road to Langley. Just four miles to the northeast on the east side of Whidbey Island, Langley boasted a deep port with daily steamship service to Everett, Seattle and Coupeville. The initial "road" to Langley, suited more to horseback riding than to buggies, had been cut through in 1891.

Also during this time roads were improved to other parts of the island. During the first two decades of the 1900s progress was made to connect Coupeville to South Whidbey by road. A wagon road was contracted in 1900 and became passable two years later. Sometime around 1910, Enoch Wood and George Mitchell, driving a Model-T Ford, completed

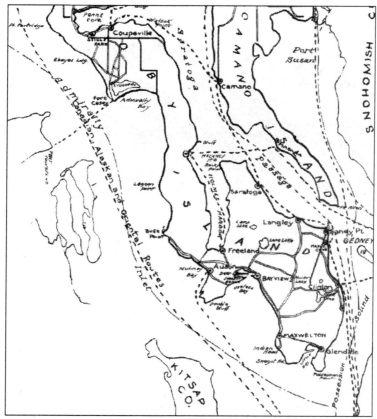

South Whidbey communities and roads around 1910.

the first trip by car along this rough road. Driving from Coupeville to Langley took them two days. By 1916 the road was graded and became fairly passable by car.[12]

Once the road opened, all travelers coming down the island passed through Bayview. At Bayview, roads branched off: northeast to Langley, east to Clinton or south to Maxwelton. Bayview became more than a corner; it became the crossroads.

Chapter 4: A Community Called "Bay View"

Automobiles on Whidbey in 1912.

As the route of commerce shifted from the high-water wharf at Bayview to Langley, farmers envisioned a new use for the large flat tidal marsh called Deer Lagoon.

---

[1] Lorna Cherry, *South Whidbey and Its People*, Vol. I, page 119.

[2] Interview with Mabel Alexander November 6, 2001.

[3] Lorna Cherry, *South Whidbey and Its People*, Vol. I, page 66.

[4] Conversation between Jan Witsoe and Dean Campbell May, 2002 reported by Jan Witsoe.

[5] The sign in front of the school gives the date 1895. I could find no evidence that the building was built at that time.

[6] Kohlwes family paper from Jan Kohlwes Witsoe.

[7] Washington School Register, District #8, 1910 to 1911.

[8] *Island County a World Beater*, 1911.

[9] Diking District Map held by Ray Gabelein, 1914.

[10] Lorna Cherry, *South Whidbey and Its People*, Vol. II, page 145.

[11] Lorna Cherry, *South Whidbey and Its People*, Vol. II, page 150.

[12] Carl Engle, *Whidbey Island Roads*, unpublished manuscript, about 1956.

Chapter 5

Bayview Becomes a Corner

Between 1900 and 1910 the population of South Whidbey increased five-fold from 331 to 1,684. Fueling this influx was the promise of farming land. However, most of the land for sale was "cutover land," tracts left after timber harvests. Such land wasn't expensive to purchase–$15-$25 per acre in 1913–and promoters claimed that just 20 acres of farmland could support a family. But it cost between $200 to $300 per acre to improve the land for farming. That cost included removing stumps and timber residue and leveling and tilling the land. Additionally, much of the cutover land consisted of gravel or clay and held little promise of even subsistence farming.

Well aware of these obstacles, the Bayview community set plans in motion to acquire farmland in an easier, less expensive way—diking. By holding back the salt water, channeling the slough and letting the marsh dry out, hundreds of flat fertile acres of land could be reclaimed for farming.

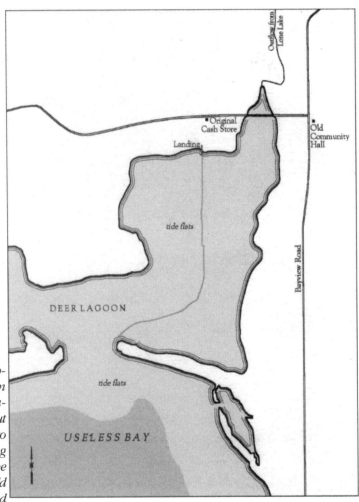

An approximation of Deer Lagoon in about 1900 prior to the diking projects. The estuary would have filled completely at high tide and emptied to tide flats and a meandering channel at low tide. At this time, the old log Community Hall stood near the present-day school. The original Cash Store was located on the wagon road, near the landing. Shallow-draft boats maneuvered up the channel to the landing at high tide.

Community at the Crossroads: The History of Bayview on Whidbey Island

Diking District #1

The plan to dike the east end of Deer Lagoon probably hatched around the wood stoves in the William Weedin and William Kohlwes kitchens. Weedin and his wife Susan had

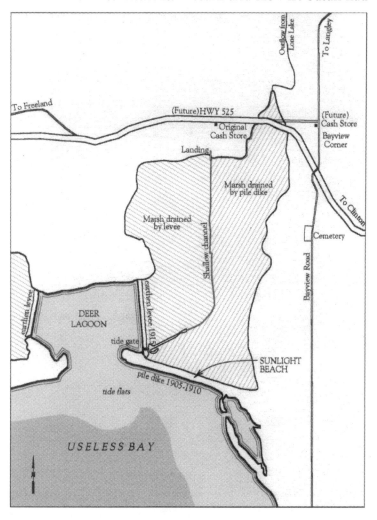

In about 1920, after several diking projects, Deer Lagoon changed dramatically. The first pile dike along Sunlight Beach and a low dirt dike north toward the landing held back the tide for a large section to the east. Later in 1915, an earthen levee closed off the rest of the estuary. The following year a second levee diked the western section of Deer Lagoon.

Chapter 5: Bayview Becomes A Corner

purchased 240 acres just south of the outfall from Lone Lake, property owned today by the Whidbey Telephone Company on Highway 525.

Originally from northern Germany, near the low country of the Netherlands, William Kohlwes and his wife Mary, whom he met in the Alaskan gold fields, arrived in Bayview in 1903. They immediately started farming their 164 acres of the original Edward Oliver property. These two families, perched on the hillside overlooking the marshy edges of Deer Lagoon, must have imagined the flat saltwater estuary producing row upon row of strawberries, vegetables and other produce. This picture was supported by the fact that between 1905 and 1910, a series of pile dikes had been built to hold back the high tide from several areas around Deer Lagoon.

Segment of a large map created in May of 1914 for Diking District #1. This map detailed the construction plan for the earthen levee on the east side of Deer Lagoon. The bottom of the map shows Sunlight Beach.

One pile dike was constructed along the Sunlight Beach sand

spit that separated Deer Lagoon and the northeast corner of Useless Bay. This dike kept high tides from washing over the sand spit and controlled the drift of sand caused by water currents in Useless Bay. A pile driver was used to install vertical poles that formed the dike.

Another pile dike inside Deer Lagoon reclaimed land north of Sunlight Beach Road and along the eastside of Deer Lagoon. The project did not affect the slough or transportation into the Bayview wharf but did prove the viability of a larger diking project.

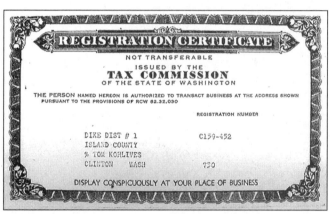

This Registration Certificate created Diking District #1 and allowed the organization to conduct business.

Earlier in 1895, the state legislature had passed laws to allow the formation of diking districts. But until 1914 no community had taken advantage of the laws, which enabled community members to organize, elect commissioners, issue bonds to build dikes and assess the landowners who would benefit. Loggers, who utilized the estuaries to store their logs, tried to keep the farmers from acting. Still the farmers persisted, and in 1914 Bayview organized the first diking district, Diking District #1.

Chapter 5: Bayview Becomes A Corner

The first meeting of Diking District #1 was on April 29, 1914. The group elected three commissioners: Herbert Weedin, son of William and Susan Weedin, was elected secretary; William Kohlwes was elected chairman; and A. F. Birkenholz was elected third commissioner. Drawings by engineer L. Wernecke were also approved for the new diking project at that first meeting.

Notes from the first meeting of the Diking District were recorded in the Diking ledger. At the first meeting on April 29, 1914, William Kohlwes was elected chairman, Herbert Weedin, secretary and A. F. Birkenholz was elected as the third commissioner.

This set in motion the plan to build a one-third-mile-long levee running north and south, which would cut off the entire east end of Deer Lagoon and open 480 acres of land to farming. Sunlight Beach spit protected the area from the fury of the open sound, making it possible to erect an earthen levee.

The project lasted from April of 1914 until May of 1915. A work force, which fluctuated between one and two dozen workers at a time, was paid 25-30 cents per hour. Raymond Gabelein, whose grandparents Emil and Emilie Gabelein had arrived in Bayview on *Howard Doe* in 1908, described the operation: *"They carved dirt from the bluff and used horses and a scraper to build the dike."*
[1] The slough was confined into one channel and flowed through a tunnel in the dike. A tide gate in the tunnel opened

to allow slough water to flow out and closed to keep the salt water out at high tide. At completion, the project created 480 acres of farmland.

The west end of Deer Lagoon toward Double Bluff was also diked with an earthen levee, creating 386 additional acres of farmland. The cost for creating farmland in this manner was approximately $100 per acre. Not only was this cheaper than clearing stumps from cutover land, but the ability to sell bonds also helped to relieve the cost to individual farmers.

The earlier pile dike along Sunlight Beach became the site of a serious accident in 1923. William Kohlwes must have been at work repairing the dike when his arm was crushed by a pile driver. The next meeting of the Diking Commission was held in an Everett hospital. At this meeting, Kohlwes gave up his position on the Diking Commission. Within one year he died from complications resulting from the accident.

The diking ledger recorded all transactions of the organization. This page from 1937 lists accounts paid for materials, labor and other expenses. Although the dikes were completed by this time, they continued to require maintenance.

During the first two decades of the 20th century, farmers tested a variety of crops in the arable lands around Deer Lagoon and Lone Lake. A. A. Terry, a recent settler to

Chapter 5: Bayview Becomes A Corner

C. G. Melendy farm in about 1910. Melendy focused his farming on poultry and fruit trees.

Bayview, raised hogs, started a dairy and planted an apple orchard. The Tiemeyer farm cultivated wheat, oats and vetch. C.G. Melendy devoted his ten acres to poultry and fruit trees. His 170 white leghorn hens produced 22,983 eggs in one year, yielding a net profit of $447.90.[2]

In the early 1900s Calista *stopped at Whidbey ports, including Langley, and transported produce to markets in Everett and Seattle.*

The Kohlwes farm raised cows, pigs, chickens and sheep. The farm's pork and veal were loaded on a boat called *Clatawa* in Langley and transported to Everett. Eggs, sour cream and produce went to Seattle via *Calista*.[3]

Mabel Alexander remembered her farm chores when she was in school in the 1930's. *"You got up in the morning and milked the cows and you separated the milk and washed those stupid separator disks and fed the calves. And then at night when you got home you did the same things all over again except you also had eggs to clean."*[4] This was no easy task since her family farm had over 1,000 laying hens.

The New Bayview Cash Store

Fire sometimes alters the course of history, but at Bayview Corner it merely accelerated a change already in progress. Since the diking of Deer Lagoon, the old wharf had become obsolete, but the Bayview Cash Store located near the wharf remained in operation. In 1916, the store at the wharf burned, and for the next eight years the community lacked a mercantile. In 1924 William Burk (later the spelling was changed to Burke) looked around his growing community and decided it was time for a new store.

After a fire destroyed the original Cash Store, a new store was built at the crossroads called Bayview Corner.

Earlier, in 1910, William Burk and his brother John had arrived in the Pacific Northwest from Arkansas. They initially worked at a mill in Seattle and then moved to Bayview and purchased the Lone Lake Mill. Lumber from this mill was used to construct houses and other buildings at Bayview. The mill burned down in 1914, and the brothers began looking for other business ventures. John built the Lone Lake Resort—11 cabins and 18 rowboats. He soon moved off the island but continued to manage the resort for 50 years.

Chapter 5: Bayview Becomes A Corner

In 1924, William Burk built a substantial new store where he sold general merchandise and farm supplies.

William Burk stayed in Bayview and constructed a substantial building to house both general merchandise and farm supplies. He kept the name of Bayview Cash Store. But foreseeing Bayview's new direction, he strategically located the store at the corner where the Langley-Clinton Road met the road that headed up island. His store soon formed both the social and geographical center of not only Bayview but also South Whidbey. Anyone going up island from Clinton or Langley had to pass through the crossroads at Bayview Corner.

William Burk didn't stay in the mercantile business for long. After six years, he sold the store to 29-year-old Harold Johnston in 1930. Harold grew up a few miles southwest of Bayview on a 40-acre farm off Lancaster Road on Double

William Burk sold his store to Harold Johnston in 1930. This photo dated July 1, 1937 shows the store crew. L to r: Harold Johnston; Howard Massey who handled the feed business; Betty Schmidt who later married Harold and Tom Ernst who had been with the store since Harold purchased it.

Bluff. After Harold's mother died, he moved to Oak Harbor to live with relatives and finish high school. There he met and married Marie Bultman, and they had two sons, Ronald and Ray. After purchasing the store, Harold moved his family into the living quarters at the back. Not only did the Cash Store become the heart of Bayview Corner, its proprietor, Harold Johnston, became one of Bayview's stalwart citizens. Shortly after the Johnstons settled into the Cash Store, Marie and Harold separated, and she returned to Oak Harbor.

From the beginning the store sold gasoline. Any traveler going up or down the island had to pass by the Cash Store, the heart of Bayview Corner.

Although Whidbey Island's population increased between the years 1900 to 1920, that trend reversed during the following decade. People left the island, drawn to increasing opportunities in the cities. When the Great Depression of the early 1930s forced people back to the island for subsistence farming, they brought their poverty with them. It was Harold Johnston who helped hold Bayview together during these hard times.

Bayview resident Carrie Ramstad Melendy remarked years ago:

I started working at the Bayview store, which was close to my home. I worked there for Harold Johnston for 26 years. For many years during the Depression of the 1930s there were a lot of people who really needed help. I know that Harold Johnston gave away food beyond what anybody realized. Boxes and boxes of groceries

Chapter 5: Bayview Becomes A Corner

went out of that Bayview store that people never did pay for because they couldn't. Frank and I were close personal friends of Harold's first wife Marie, so we knew what was going on.[5]

Harold continued to run the store during the difficult 1930s and even expanded it. In 1937, he celebrated with a grand reopening. The local newspaper, the Whidbey Record, dedicated much of its July 29, 1937, issue to wishing Johnston success:

The Whidbey Record devoted most of one issue in 1937 to the grand reopening of the newly remodeled Cash Store.

Originally the Bay View Cash Store occupied only the small front with the large show windows. The large feed warehouses to the left were added during the last three years. This last spring the main store portion was extended back to occupy twice the space formerly used for merchandising.

Taken over by Harold B. Johnston in 1930 at the first of one the country's worst periods of depression, the institution has forged steadily ahead under the wise merchandising policies of its owner until today it occupies the enviable place of one of the largest mercantile establishments on Whidbey Island.

Located in the center of one of South Whidbey's finest farming areas and at an important cross roads, the institution serves a large local and transient trade. The store's policies of fair dealing and service bring it customers from all over the South End and as far north as Coupeville. [6]

The newspaper listed items available at the Cash Store: fresh and tinned food, cheese, brooms, cleaning supplies and sundries. Motor oil, gasoline, hip boots, dynamite and hay were sold. As an additional business, Harold sold and installed pumps for wells.

The grand reopening of the Cash Store called for some special deals for customers.

Chapter 5: Bayview Becomes A Corner

The operation of the newly remodeled store didn't consume all of Harold Johnston's time. Somewhere between the cash register and the pickle barrel, love blossomed. Elizabeth (Betty) Schmidt, who had been living with a relative in Portland, Oregon, returned to the island in 1934 and took a job in the store. In 1938 Harold and Betty were married and four years later their daughter Judy was born.

Bayview Hall

In 1927 the Bayview community joined together again, this time to build Bayview Hall. They envisioned a place for Saturday night dances, meetings of fraternal organizations, wedding anniversaries, musical troupes and

Betty Schmidt and Harold Johnston were married on January 8, 1938. This photo taken on their wedding day shows the couple prepared to leave for their honeymoon.

Betty Schmidt Johnston started this dairy in January of 1938 and wrote daily for over five years. She noted the many visitors to their home, the activities of her family and friends and special events at Bayview Corner.

Community at the Crossroads: The History of Bayview on Whidbey Island

Bayview Hall was completed in 1928. This photo shows the hall across the corn field that separated it from the Cash Store.

community plays. They hoped to serve all of South Whidbey and even attract folks from Coupeville.

The community incorporated as the Whidby Community Hall Association (the official name omitted the "e" in the word Whidbey). Herbert Weedin, whose farm extended from Deer Lagoon marsh near the old wharf up toward the road to Clinton, donated the land for the hall. This small lot was south of the Cash Store, just beyond William Burk's cornfield. Burk, who hadn't sold the Cash Store yet, contributed the nails.

Frank Olsen, who lived at the foot of Brooks Hill Road, became the project's chief carpenter. Olsen designed the building and was paid a salary—about $2 per day—by the association. The other workers volunteered their services. A list of the workers includes both early Bayview names and newer people who had arrived at Bayview during the first decades of the century. They included Frank Olsen, John Josephson,

Chapter 5: Bayview Becomes A Corner

Charles Farrell, Clifford Thompson, the Kohlwes brothers, Harold Johnston, Frank Melendy, Felix Gabelein, the Jewetts and the Petersons.[7]

To finance the building of the hall, the Whidby Community Hall Association sold bonds for $25. One hundred and fifty bonds were sold, but none were ever redeemed.

To finance the project, the association sold 150 utility bonds to pay for lumber. Each $25 bond paid interest at two percent per annum. The association gave Herbert Weedin four $25 bonds for his land donation and later issued bonds to workers for their labor.

The first step in the construction of the hall was digging a well in the basement for water. The mostly volunteer workforce started on the construction of the building, utilizing local old-growth wood. A stage took shape at one end of the long interior and a second-story balcony with wooden benches encircled the two long sides and rear. William Kohlwes' son Fred and farmer Frank Melendy installed electrical wires and a gas engine, which produced electricity. The hall had electricity 16 years before Puget Power brought power to the area. But the pride and joy of the Bayview builders was the wooden dance floor. Fine-grained maple boards were installed and sanded smooth for dancing. We can imagine the community celebration when the hall first opened.

Once the hall opened, the Whidby Community Hall Association continued to operate it. Oscar Thompson, who lived and farmed west of Bayview, served as the first manager and held the position for many years. Income from ticket sales paid for the hall's upkeep and interest on the building bonds. There is no record that anyone ever redeemed any bonds for payment, and no one can remember doing so.

The Langley High School dances were held at Bayview Hall

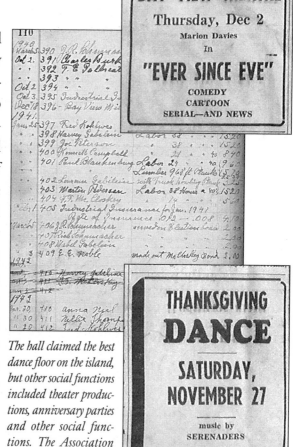

The hall claimed the best dance floor on the island, but other social functions included theater productions, anniversary parties and other social functions. The Association continued to manage the hall. Fees for use offset expenses as shown in this page from the hall ledger.

and Lucille Thompson Nourse remembered them well. She was a high school student in the early 1940s. *"We had the junior prom and the senior ball always at the hall. For the junior prom they would parade, boy-girl, and it was so pretty because all the girls would have their long dresses on and promenade. All the grandmas and grandpas would come and sit upstairs and the folks too, always the whole family. This was a community affair."* 8

The community feeling didn't stop at the door of Bayview Hall. Mabel Olsen Alexander remembered sharing their family's produce with others in the community. *"My sister and I on Saturdays we'd catch a bunch of fish and take them to all the bachelors that lived around the lake. One place we'd get a banana, at another hard candy or a cookie. We didn't think a thing of going in to the old bachelors and sit and talkin'. We never worried. Those were the good old days."* 9

By 1930 Bayview Corner had assumed its present shape. The three major public buildings—the Cash Store, Bayview Hall and Bayview School—showcased an active community. The Corner looked to Langley as a port, where steamers carrying passengers and goods on Puget Sound from Oak Harbor to Seattle regularly stopped. Also, there was talk of connecting South Whidbey to the mainland with regular car ferry service between Columbia Beach and Mukilteo. Bayview Corner was to become even busier when the island opened to a new wave of invaders: tourists.

[1] Interview with Ray Gabelein, October 15, 2001.

[2] *Island County a World Beater*, Page 10-11.

[3] Kohlwes family papers from Jan Kohlwes Witsoe.

[4] Interview with Mabel Olsen Alexander, November 6, 2001.

[5] Lorna Cherry, *South Whidbey and Its People, Vol. II*, page 151.

[6] The Whidbey Record, Thursday, July 29, 1937.

[7] Lorna Cherry, *South Whidbey and Its People, Vol. II*, page 139.

[8] Interview with Lucile Thompson Nourse, November 6, 2001.

[9] Interview with Mabel Olsen Alexander and Lucile Thompson Nourse, November 6, 2001.

Chapter 6

Bayview Corner Grows

Regular car ferry service between Mukilteo on the mainland and Columbia Beach (now referred to as Clinton) at the south end of Whidbey Island began in the mid-1920s. Part way up the island, the Keystone- to- Port Townsend Ferry linked Whidbey to the Olympic Peninsula in 1927. A bridge spanning Deception Pass on the extreme north end of Whidbey was completed in 1935. These three new mainland ties brought both visitors who came for recreation and permanent residents who came to farm and provide services.

Chapter 6: Bayview Corner Grows

Cars waiting at the Columbia Beach dock to take the ferry to Mukilteo. Photo 1935.

The auto ferries lured day and weekend tourists from Everett and Seattle. Sportsmen hunted deer, duck, quail and pheasant, and they fished when salmon runs filled the waters around Whidbey. Special Sunday Whidbey auto tours were advertised in Seattle newspapers, which brought families to picnic, play on the beach and relax. Camping became popular. Soon cabins and guest cottages sprouted for tourists to rent. Salmon barbecues, clam bakes and crab feeds—food gleaned from the shores around Useless Bay— created festive family times. Beach bonfires lingered into the evening as adults shared stories and kids played kick-the-can in the darkening shadows.

Children on dock at Sunlight Beach. Photo taken before 1911.

Lucille Thompson (Nourse) and Dick Simmonson celebrate their birthdays in 1932 with Bayview friends. Front row left to right: Alberta Gabelein, Eileen Gabelein, Mabel Olsen, Maxine Ulrich, Lucille Thompson, Alvina Gabelein, Helen Blankenberg. Back row left to right: Junius Hagglund, Raynard Gabelein, Herman Hagglund, Don Simmonson, Dick Simmonson, Raymond Gabelein, Leo Jensen, Roland Quigley, Jim Thompson.

When William and Mary Kohlwes bought their 164 acres in 1903, they acquired the sandy strip of beachfront between Useless Bay and Deer Lagoon. Focused on farming and unaware of the potential value of beach property, the Kohlwes family sold the sand spit in 1913 for $1,500 to Billy Hofer and Chancy Wernecke. They dubbed the area Sunlight Beach, promoted camping and bragged about the warm, safe water for swimming. Wernecke and Hofer sold lots 50 feet wide on Useless Bay and 100 feet deep. Later John and Charlotte Thompson built cabins on the beach, which they rented to summer vacationers.

Billy Hofer who, along with Chancy Wernecke, purchased the sand spit and developed Sunlight Beach. Photo 1931.

Chapter 6: Bayview Corner Grows

John and Charlotte Thompson rented out cabins on Sunlight Beach.

The Bayview community enthusiastically welcomed these visitors. Arlene Kohlwes Alschbauch-Scott, granddaughter of William and Mary Kohlwes, was raised on the family farm above Sunlight Beach and remembered selling milk, eggs, strawberries, cherries and raspberries to the summer people. *"My mother Clara made cakes and sold them to the folks on the beach."* [1]

Frederick Kohlwes is holding Alfred, and his wife Clara is holding daughter Arlene.

Strawberry fields on the old Kohlwes farm.

The Kohlwes orchard included acres of filbert trees. In this photo women are gathering the filbert nuts off the ground.

Fishing resorts sprouted near the shores and lured tourists for salmon fishing. However, commercial fishing with fish traps and fish wheels reduced the opportunities for sport fishermen. In 1934, sporting organizations, including the Holmes Harbor Rod and Gun Club, backed an initiative to ban fish traps and fish wheels. Passage of the initiative put restraints on commercial fishing and left more salmon for recreational fishing. Other measures reserved sections of beaches for non-commercial shellfish collection, which also added to the appeal for tourists.

The increased tourist activity kept Harold Johnston's Cash Store busy. The term "Cash Store," however, was simply wishful thinking on the part of Johnston. From the beginning, patrons shopped at the store or received groceries delivered at home and then paid their bills at the end of the month

Betty Schmidt Johnston is holding a 17 pound salmon.

Chapter 6: Bayview Corner Grows

Although the store was called the Cash Store, most patrons put their purchases on an account and paid at the end of the month. These receipts were found recently when the Cash Store was remodeled.

or whenever they could. By the 1960s, the store held accounts for more than 1,500 customers.

During the early 1940s Harold's oldest son Ron, while also attending high school and assisting at the store, was responsible for three delivery routes by truck. *"One went north into Langley, which wasn't bad because I could pick up fresh butterhorns at the Langley bakery. The delivery route west to Mutiny Bay allowed me to stop and shoot ducks on the water. The third route south served the permanent residents and summer folks down on Sunlight Beach Road."* [2]

Successful hunters are standing at the back of the Cash Store near where the Smilin' Dog Café is today. Left to right: Mike O'Leary, Harold Johnston, Harold's sons Ron and Ray and Howard Massey. The dog's name was Queenie.

When fishing was good, Ron's dad often kept the store open on Saturday nights and left Ron in charge, a downside of working for his dad. Fishermen came in to pick up bait and beer late at night so they could start fishing early in the morning. Ron would rather have been enjoying the teen dances at Bayview Hall. On one occasion his younger brother Ray had to pick up Ron's girlfriend before a dance.[3]

The interior of the Cash Store with workers and patrons.

Open all day and often into the evening, the Cash Store, located across the street from the Bayview School, also attracted local young people. A large extended family of Johnstons, many of whom worked and sometimes lived at the back of the store, kept the activity level high. Harold and Betty embraced parents and children and made the store a welcome place to visit and linger.

Raymond Gabelein, grandson of Emil and Emilie Gabelein and one year younger than Ron Johnston,

Looking at the Cash Store from the south showing the Johnston's living quarters on the right and old garage on the left.

Chapter 6: Bayview Corner Grows

has fond memories of the store. High school students waiting to catch the school bus to Langley huddled around the stove. Raymond also recalled the time Harold Johnston, *"piled the baseball team in his Model-T pick up and hauled us all to play ball at another school."* Raymond described Johnston as, *"like a banker. When I bought my first tractor he loaned me money. When I went to pay him part of what I owed him, he asked me if I wanted a receipt. I said, 'What good does a receipt do, Harold? You don't have anything to show that I owe you money.'"*

Shopping at the Bayview Cash Store.

Wedding photo of Carrie and Frank Melendy. She worked at the Cash Store for many years. Photo taken September 12, 1926.

Judy Johnston Thorsen, the caboose of the family, was born in 1942 when Ron was eighteen. She remembered the potbelly stove and riding her tricycle around the store. Hazel Watkins and Carrie Melendy, long-time employees of the store, were like second mothers to her.

Hazel Watkins worked at the store for 23 years beginning in 1947. She remembered big rounds of cheese that Harold bought, aged and sold to customers. *"Once a customer tasted our cheese, they always came back."* Ice cream was also a hit at only ten cents for a double scoop.[4]

Looking at Bayview Corner from the school yard. The Cash Store is on the left and the Grimm's Garage on the right.

Gradually, the road system around South Whidbey expanded, opening access to waterfront areas. By 1935 Island County had 325 miles of paved roads, the majority located on Whidbey. The Cash Store responded to increased auto traffic by selling gas from pumps installed at the corner. Around 1930, Fred Grimm built and operated a car repair garage across from the Cash Store.

As the Cash Store prospered, other businesses were attracted to the locale. Prior to 1930, the Kash Inn opened just across from the Cash Store and west of Grimm's Garage. The two-story inn had rooms for rent upstairs, but locals recall it being more of a drinking establishment than an inn. Many teetotaling Scandinavians claimed they never crossed

To the north and west of the Cash Store stood the Kash Inn, a tavern with rooms to rent upstairs.

the threshold. Mabel Olsen Alexander, Scandinavian roots notwithstanding, not only entered the building, but attended Lutheran catechism confirmation classes there. There was no Lutheran minister at the time. *"We had confirmation classes at the school, after school was out for the day. But a couple times we met at the apartment above the Kash Inn, because it was right handy there at school. You might say, I had confirmation classes in a tavern by a German Methodist minister."*[6] In 1943 the building burned and the inn closed.

Another business joined Bayview Corner for a much longer tenure. The Whidbey Telephone Company started serving customers in 1908 from its first office in Langley. In 1953, 23-year-old David Henny purchased the company

The Whidbey Telephone Company started in 1908 in Langley. This photo shows Vera Rothgeb working in the telephone office prior to 1911. She had ten "out lines" with ten parties each.

and immediately began to increase service and customers. By 1960 the company had outgrown its Langley office and was in need of additional space and a more central location. Henny chose the location of the old Weedin farm near the site of the original wharf where a century earlier, boats first found their way to the Bayview Community.

> **SUDDEN ILLNESS**
>
> In the early morning hours, or when you are home alone... are you prepared to summon quick aid in case of sudden illness? With a telephone in your home your physician is only a few minutes away. You owe it to your family to have this economical protection for the sake of safety as well as convenience. Write or call us today for complete information on installing a phone in your home.
>
> **Whidby Telephone Co.**
> Serving South Whidby
> The Clock Around

This advertisement by the Whidbey Telephone Company ran in the Whidbey Record of 1937.

David Henny, a telephone tinkerer from the age of 12, set about giving his customers excellent service and state-of-the-art technology. His company was the first in the continental United States to have 100 percent buried cable. Henny himself covered the switchboard on Christmas and Mother's Day to give his employees the time off. Henny's wife Marion recalled: *"Back in the 1960s sometimes customers paid their bill with eggs. Once we even received a long, purple limousine as payment. We called it the 'Lima Bean' and could haul all our seven kids and even more."* [7] Since emergency calls for help came through the phone company, David and Marion Henny were often the first to hear about needs in the community. In the 1970s they opened the old Weedin farmhouse as a "Help House," a temporary place for the homeless or people in crisis.

Chapter 6: Bayview Corner Grows

The Whidbey Telephone Company as it looks today. David Henny established the practice of flying the American flag both day and night.

I asked Marion about the huge American flag that flies day and night above the phone company buildings. *"David was very patriotic and wanted that flag. It was the biggest we could get."* [8]

Social activities at Bayview Hall thrived. A projection booth and equipment to show movies were installed. Special social events, funerals, traveling bands and school Christmas pageants filled the weekends. Community dances were the big draw when on Saturday nights young and old gathered to dance and socialize.

The Whidby Community Hall Association Board continued to be responsible for the hall, but appointed managers to handle the day-to-day operations. Oscar Thompson managed the hall for many years beginning in 1928. Management passed through several hands during the 1940s to the 1960s. In the 1940s the Holmes Harbor Rod and Gun Club took over the management. Raymond Gabelein remembered attending dances as a young man. *"Usually a fight or two broke out behind the hall."* Eventually, the dances changed from events that the whole community attended to dances for teens.

Performance in the Bayview Hall.

Years later, when his own children began frequenting the dances in the 1960s, Raymond and his wife Eva Mae assumed management responsibility for the hall, a position they held for nearly 30 years. In the 1960s the dances were attracting young people from all over the island as well as from Seattle. Raymond Gabelein remembered, *"We had to hire the band and get chaperones. We set the limit at 500 people, and still they lined up outside the door. Only when one person came out did we let more in. We had to set the rules. If they went out they couldn't come back. We didn't want them drinking in the parking lot and then coming back."*

This interior photo from the upstairs at Bayview Hall shows the balconies on each side and the stage at the far end.

Eva Mae continued, *"First the dances cost $2, then we raised it to $4. We paid the band $500. Our younger kids sold hot dogs, candy and pop in the basement. Raymond became a deputy sheriff to run those dances for the hall. We organized the dances for about 15 years."* [9]

Jan Kohlwes Witsoe, granddaughter of William and Mary Kohlwes, clearly remembered those teen dances and the boys that came from the Ballard area of Seattle. *"The dances were very popular, lots of kids came from in town. That's where I met the Ballard Boys. We all dated the Ballard Boys, and three of us married them."* [10]

When Skagit Valley Community College requested to hold a grocery checking class in the hall, they had the building inspected first. The inspectors pronounced the hall very sound, and Raymond Gabelein agreed with their findings. *"[There's] all old growth lumber in that hall. If you go down in the basement it's just as sound as it can be. You won't see a termite in that hall. Termites don't like old growth, they just like second growth."* [11]

During the nearly thirty years when the Gabeleins managed the hall, a new water system was connected and the old well discontinued. Around 1969, the Association purchased land next to the hall for $2,500 in order to install a septic system. A new roof was put on the hall and paid for in 1995. Evidently there were some folks who got busted for pot that needed to do community service, so they installed the roof to pay off their hours.

While the Cash Store prospered and the Bayview Hall attracted people from far and wide, a different kind of change occurred at Bayview School. After serving the elementary school population for almost 50 years, the Bayview School closed its doors in 1942 when the South Whidbey School District consolidated the kindergarten to eighth grade students into one elementary school in Langley. Other local schools, including Intervale on Maxwelton Road, were part of the consolidation. The Bayview community

A class photo of the Bayview School in 1937. Although other schools consolidated as early as 1935, Bayview remained open until 1942.

strongly resisted the move, but could not hold back the tides of change. Eva Mae Gabelein, a member of the last class to graduate from Bayview School, recalled: *"Prior to consolidation there were four grades in one room with one teacher and four grades in another. The janitor started the fire in the furnace in the basement and the teacher kept it going."* [12]

One reason given by the school district for closing down the rural schools was that it wasn't possible to get a good education at a small school with more than one grade in a room. Eva Mae proved them wrong. After attending eight grades at Bayview School she went on to high school and became salutatorian of her graduating class. The valedictorian of the class was also from one of the small schools closed down for consolidation.

The Bayview School bell now hangs in a new structure in front of the schoolhouse.

The large school building remained in good shape, and several local organizations used the building for various activities. The American Legion occupied the building prior to the Skagit Valley Community College. In 1995, an alternative school for high school aged students now called Bayview School, moved into the historic building.

The most intriguing Bayview School story is the 40-year saga of the school bell. Raymond Gabelein told me this version. The large cast iron bell happily hung in its belfry until the school closed down. The bell was removed and stored in the basement. During the time the American Legion used the school building, concern grew that the bell would be damaged or perhaps removed by the Legion and sold. Raymond Gabelein and others removed the bell for "safe keeping" and housed it, without telling anyone, in Ray's barn. It sat there quietly for a decade or so. One year some folks asked to use the bell in a parade at the Island County Fair in Langley, so Gabelein consented. However, the bell was not returned to Gabelein but instead hidden in Andy Anderson's woods. Wandering through the woods one day, Raymond stumbled on the bell and brought it back to his house.

A few years later the bell was moved again, this time to Langley High School where it was used as a victory bell. However, the bell was left out at the High School, and concern mounted about the future of the bell. About this time Raymond ran across a newspaper article about another school consolidation where the ownership of the school bell was contested. In that case, the bell was awarded to the local school not the district. Armed with determination and this article, Raymond kept voicing his concerns. In the early 1990s several community members and the school superintendent Lisa Bjork gathered forces to reinstall the bell at the Bayview School. Finally, in 1995 the old bell rang again at the Bayview School. A community gathering celebrated its return.

Chapter 6: Bayview Corner Grows

This 1950s aerial photo shows Bayview Corner prior to the construction of Highway 525. All traffic went north on Bayview Road and turned left at the Cash Store.

School consolidation foreshadowed a more significant event involving Bayview Corner. In the late 1950s the Island's main road, which started at the Clinton ferry dock and traveled up island to Deception Pass Bridge, was improved and straightened. Instead of following Bayview Road to Bayview Corner, the new road now bypassed Bayview Corner to the southwest. Years before, the Diking District took the Bayview from Bayview Corner, and now the highway department removed the corner.

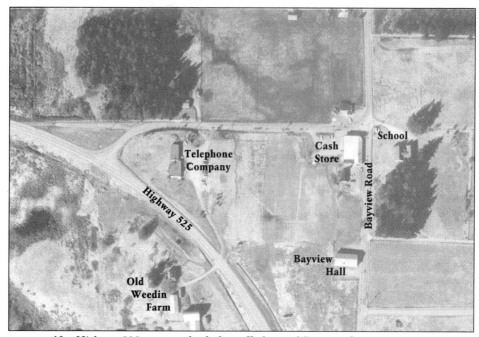
After Highway 525 was completed, the traffic bypassed Bayview Corner.

The teen dances remained popular and Harold Johnston continued to run the Cash Store. But he and Betty spent more and more time traveling and gradually Bayview Corner and the rest of South Whidbey slumped into a quiet period. Jan Kohlwes Witsoe remembered that time: "The whole island seemed to close up in the late 1960s. The Clyde Theater in Langley closed. I don't remember there being a restaurant in Langley. The young people all wanted to move away and get off the rock."[13]

Chapter 6: Bayview Corner Grows

[1] Interview with Arlene Alschbauch-Scott, October 25, 2001.

[2] Bayview Live: Stories as Told by our Seniors. Part one. Recorded September 23, 2001.

[3] Bayview Live: Stories as Told by our Seniors. Part one. Recorded September 23, 2001.

[4] Interview with Eva Mae and Raymond Gabelein, October 14, 2001.

[5] Bayview Live: Stories as Told by our Seniors. Part one. Recorded September 23, 2001.

[6] Interview with Mabel Alexander, November 6, 2001.

[7] Interview with Marion Henny, August 19, 2002.

[8] Interview with Marion Henny, August 19, 2002.

[9] Interview with Eva Mae and Raymond Gabelein, October 14, 2001.

[10] Interview with Janet Witsoe, October 25, 2001.

[11] Interview with Eva Mae and Raymond Gabelein, October 14, 2001.

[12] Interview with Eva Mae and Raymond Gabelein, October 14, 2001.

[13] Interview with Janet Witsoe, October 25, 2001.

Chapter 7

Bayview Corner Revived

The highway whisked visitors past the Bayview Corner as it continued its slumber through the 1970s, 80s and into the 90s. Somehow the corner managed to avoid the strip mall development and modernizing that happened in other parts of Whidbey. The rural character of the corner hung on like a comfortable old shoe.

Harold Johnston sold the Cash Store in 1975 to Jack and Grace Cortes. Ten years later it changed hands again, this time to Bill Lanning Jr. who restored the exterior and remodeled the interior. Lanning lived in the back two-story apartment and operated Bill's Feed and Tack up front. There he sold jeans, shirts, tools, animal feed and baby chicks. He leased part of the front room to Whidbey Island Food Co-op.

Established in 1996, the Smilin' Dog Café provides coffee, food and a place to linger and read the paper.

In 1991, Lanning moved out of the apartment and leased the back space to Jonni Reed, who opened an antique store named "Findings." Jonni's longhaired dachshund, named Sudi, accompanied her to the store. After a few years in the antique business, Jonni relocated her shop upstairs and opened a coffee shop downstairs. Now Sudi had to stay home. But each day when Jonni returned home from work, her dog was waiting for her and smiling. When Jonni opened her coffee shop on April 6, 1996, Jonni named it The Smilin' Dog.

Bill Lanning sold the building in 1994 to Don Azar. Along with Lanning's departure went the feed and tack store; a bicycle shop, art store and gallery grew in its place. Azar also bought the land to the southwest where Maureen and Jim Rowley opened a nursery called Bayview Farm and Garden.

The Bayview School building houses the alternative school for South Whidbey high school students. The original bell was reinstalled in front.

The Bayview School building took on new life in September 1995 when an alternative school for South Whidbey high school students moved in. The school, called simply Bayview School, opened with 47 students and director, Joy Kawasaki.

The Bayview Hall continued to hold Saturday night contra dances, special parties and anniversaries. Now the board of directors of the Whidby Community Hall Association handles the business. Anyone in the community

A sign welcomes visitors to the businesses at Bayview Corner.

can join the Association for $5; members receive the group's newsletter.

In 1998 some folks with new ideas began sniffing around Bayview Corner. "My involvement started with a conversation in the parking lot," recalled Nancy Nordhoff, president of the Goosefoot Community Fund. "I knew Linda Moore slightly and we got to talking about preserving the building and some land around it." Over the next year they formed the Goosefoot Community Fund, financed by Nancy Nordoff. The Fund purchased the Cash Store and 19 acres on both sides of Bayview Road north of Highway 525. Redevelopment of the corner began in 1999 and continues into the fall of 2002 as this is written. Plans

New businesses are fitting nicely into the historic buildings at Bayview Corner. Bayview Arts is housed in the building on the left. The Smilin' Dog Café is on the right, located in the old Cash Store building.

are underway to complete the preservation and remodeling of the Cash Store.

Recently an even older structure has joined the trio of historic buildings. A 1914 Sears and Roebuck house had been lifted from its original location at the Loganberry Farm in Greenbank. The Goosefoot Community Fund received permission by the board of the Greenbank Farm to move the Sears house to a permanent site on the eastside of Bayview Road. The building was carefully restored retaining as much of the original structure as possible. Today, with a new foundation and daylight basement, it houses the offices of the Whidbey Camano Land Trust and Flat Rock Productions.

Recently the 1914 Sears house was relocated to Bayview. Redwood salvaged from the old Langley Water Tower was remilled and used for ceiling, wainscotting and other architectural detailing in the house.

Moving the Sears house initiated some out-of-the-box thinking around the Goosefoot office coffee machine and resulted in another activity of the group. The conversation must have started something like this: "Why don't we offer to move the summer houses and smaller beach cabins that are slated for demolition and use them to provide affordable housing?"

Off the wall idea? Absolutely. But that's what happened. The Goosefoot Affordable Housing Program sprang into life to recycle unwanted houses and assist local families in obtaining affordable housing. It keeps those houses from the landfill and also preserves the rural character of Island County. To date six houses have been moved. Goosefoot also provides technical assistance and bridge financing to the recipients.

Goosefoot's Community Loan Fund was established to help with house financing and other capital needs for local businesses. It offers below-market capital and gives technical assistance for economic development of local businesses, sustainable development technologies and affordable housing.

As Goosefoot continues to redevelop Bayview Corner, it maintains high standards of sustainable building practices. When a new foundation was needed under the Cash Store, each old floorboard was carefully removed and later put back in place. The public restroom consists of composting toilets and waterless urinals. An old garage was restored into Bayview Arts, an art supply and gift shop. Not only does the corner model sustainable building practices, it

Bayview Arts is housed in the old garage. The large bat house on top was installed to encourage the local bat colony out of the attic of the old Cash Store and into these delux new quarters.

offers this expertise to the community through workshops, special events and informational displays and materials.

Fundamental in the redevelopment activities at Bayview Corner is the collaboration and cooperation with its neighbors: Bayview School, Bayview Farm and Garden, Bayview Hall and Whidbey Telephone Company.

On Saturdays from spring through fall, the Bayview Farmers' Market transforms the Corner's parking lot between the Cash Store building and the Bayview Hall into a festive town square. Locals gather to purchase fresh vegetables, flowers, home baked food items and to run into their neighbors. More than 50 local vendors make up the Bayview Farmers' Market, an independent non-profit organization.

Fanciful signs direct visitors to the Bayview Corner businesses.

These varied projects, businesses and collaborations continue to reinforce Goosefoot's themes and goals: to establish Bayview Corner as a place that is grounded in Whidbey's rural past; to be a commercial crossroads open to, supporting, and encouraging a diverse community; and to be a model of down-to-earth environmentally sound products and practices. Goosefoot now has an active Board of Directors who will carry on in this spirit.

Chapter 7: Bayview Corner Revived

When Thomas Johns and Edward Oliver first laid eyes on the Bayview area almost 150 years ago, they had a dream. Their vision for homes, a school and businesses shaped a community.

Three main legacies of the early community survive. The Cash Store supplies food and goods, Bayview School offers a better future for our children and Bayview Hall remains a venue for community gatherings. Real community happens when locals know each other, when they work and play together.

So next time you are driving up Highway 525, stop at the Bayview Road traffic light and turn right toward Bayview Corner. Spend some time snooping, get a cup of coffee, sit on a bench and enjoy a few minutes of wool gathering. Imagine Edward Oliver—blond hair flowing, blue eyes shining—as he clambered off his boat, scrambled up the bank and decided, "Yep, this is it!"

Chapter 7: Bayview Corner Revived

Chronology

1822   William T. Johnson was born.

1839   Edward Oliver was born in Virginia.

1840   Thomas Johns was born in Plymouth, England.

1858   Edward Oliver came to Deer Lagoon and settled south of Sunlight Beach. (Date approximate.) Probably ran a logging camp for 10 years.

1859   Thomas Johns deserted the English Navy, came to Deer Lagoon and settled north of Sunlight Beach. Joined Oliver in logging enterprise.

1866   William Tiemeyer bought 164 acres near Sunlight Beach from Edward Oliver. Later expanded holdings to 400 acres.

1869   William T. Johnson "settled" land on Double Bluff that probably came from wife Jane Newbury, a Snohomish Indian.

1872   Thomas Johns filed intention to buy land on the east side of Deer Lagoon.

1872   James Phinney homesteaded 130 acres on the southwestern side of Deer Lagoon.

1873   William Johnson bought 153.65 acres on Double Bluff, probably same land that he settled in 1869.

1874   Thomas Johns married Mary Jane Coffelt on Lopez Island.

1874   Robert Ware homesteaded 160 acres northeast of Deer Lagoon. Later added to his holdings making a total of 240 acres. The land was broken up and sold to Frank and Carrie Melendy, Mr. and Mrs. F. F. McCloskey, George and Hazel Watkins, Fred and Sylvia Grimm, Mr. and Mrs. A. B. Kramer. Part of this piece became the Herbert Weedin farm.

1874   Edward Oliver purchased 164 acres overlooking Sunlight Beach, later owned by William and Mary Kohlwes.

1875   William Johnson who homesteaded 160 acres at Double Bluff, now owns 313 acres.

1877   George Finn purchased 120 acres near Double Bluff from Edward Oliver and Thomas Johns.

1877   George Finn married Catherine, a Snohomish Indian.

1877   Edward Oliver married Melvinia Sooy, part Snohomish Indian. (Date approximate.)

1880   Old log Community Hall built. (Date approximate.)

1886 Name "Bay View" was in common use.

1886 Bayview School opened in temporary housing.

1886 William Johnson died in boat.

1886 Melvinia Oliver died.

1887 Edward Oliver married Jane Johnson. Oliver moved to Jane Johnson's property on Double Bluff.

1889 Washington became a state.

1892 Road from Bayview to Langley completed.

1892 Road from South Whidbey to Coupeville surveyed.

1905 Bayview Cemetery designated.

1906 William and Christine Dow bought 25 acres from Edward Oliver on the Mutiny Bay side of Double Bluff and became close neighbors.

1908 Population of South Whidbey was 1,603.

1908 Original Cash Store built at the wharf. (Date approximate.)

1908 Bayview School building opened. (Date approximate.)

1914 Diking project on east side of Deer Lagoon.

Chronology

1915   Diking project on west side of Deer Lagoon.

1916   Original Cash Store at the wharf burned.

1924   William Burk built the Cash Store.

Mid-
1920s Columbia Beach-to-Mukilteo ferry opened.

1927   Keystone-to-Port Townsend ferry opened.

1928   Bayview Hall opened.

1930   Harold Johnston purchased Cash Store.

1935   Deception Pass Bridge opened.

1937   Grand reopening of Bayview Cash Store.

Resources

Books, Booklets and Manuscripts:

Cherry, Lorna *South Whidbey and Its People Volume I.* Langley, Washington, South Whidbey Historical Society, 1983.

Cherry, Lorna *South Whidbey and Its People Volume II.* Langley, Washington, South Whidbey Historical Society, 1985.

Cherry, Lorna *Langley, The Village by the Sea, South Whidbey and Its People Volume III.* Langley, Washington, South Whidbey Historical Society, 1986.

Engle, Carl "Whidbey Island Roads," 1957 (unpublished).

Harmon, Alexandra *Indians in the Making, Ethnic Relations and Indian Identities around Puget Sound.* Berkeley: University of California Press, 1998.

Island County Historical Society *Sails, Steamships & Sea Captains: Settlement, Trade and Transportation of Island County between 1850-1900.* Coupeville, Washington, 1993.

Island County Historical Society *Bow to Plow: Timber-Tillage and Taters Agriculture and Logging in Island County 1850-1920.* Coupeville, Washington, 1995.

Kellogg, George A. *A History of Whidbey's Island.* Coupeville, Washington, Island County Historical Society, 1934.

Ryan, Helene *A Boy in Paradise, A centennial look at the boy who became the father of Langley.* Langley, Washington, South Whidbey Historical Society, 1999.

South Whidbey Historical Society *Island County a World Beater.* Langley, Washington, 1968.

White, Richard *Land Use, Environment, and Social Change: The Shaping of Island County, Washington.* Seattle: University of Washington Press, 1980.

Newspapers and Magazines:

South Whidbey Record, (also called Whidbey Record) Langley, Washington. July 29, 1937, November 30, 1939.

Spindrift Magazine, "Old News from South Whidbey." Spring, 1996.

Spindrift Magazine, "Tales of Early South Whidbey." Summer, 1998.

Spindrift Two, "South Whidbey History Told in News Clips." Spring, 1989.

Additional Resources:

Bayview Live: Stories as Told by our Seniors, Parts 1, 2, 3, and 4.
    Radio programs produced by Goosefoot Community Fund, Bayview, Washington, Fall, 2001.

Taped interviews with the following people were very useful in completing this book. Whether quoted or not, their stories contributed greatly to discovering the history of Bayview:
    Alexander, Mabel Olsen
    Alschbauch-Scott, Arlene Kohlwes
    Baker, Leda
    Burke, Art and Dorothy
    Gabelein, Eva Mae and Raymond
    Johnston, Fran
    Johnston, Ron
    Josephson, Nora and Harry
    Kohlwes, Karen and Bob
    Kohlwes, Mae Stone
    Henny, Marion
    Nordhoff, Nancy
    Nourse, Lucille Thompson
    Thorsen, Judy Johnston
    Saunders, Maxine
    Witsoe, Jan Kohlwes
    Varon, Evelyn Hagstrom

Photo, Graphic and Map Credits

Fortunately many community members contributed photos for this project, unfortunately the source of some of the photos was not recorded. Where known we attribute credit. For the unacknowledged photos, I apologize and thank you all.

Christopher Baldwin: 1, (all except upper left), 3, 4, 6, 7, 8, 35, 36 (both), 46, 47, 54, 55, 56 (bottom photos), 58, 59, 68 (top), 73, 74, 76, 78, 83 (center and bottom), 85, 86 (bottom), 87, 88, 89.

Burke family: front cover (left), 29.

Flat Rock Productions: 14, 44, 45.

Johnston family: front cover (top right and bottom right), 19 (upper right), 23, 43, 52 (top and bottom), 53, 56 (top photo), 57 (bottom), 67(bottom), 68 (bottom), 69 (both), 70 (top), 71, 72 (top).

Kohlwes family: 38 (bottom), 66 (center and bottom), 67 (top), 75.

Lucille Thompson Nourse: 43 (center), 63 (center), 65 (top).

South Whidbey Historical Society: front cover (center right), 9, (photos only), 19, (all except upper right), 21, 24, 25, 27, 28, 31, 32,34, 37 (top and bottom), 38 (top), 39 (top and bottom), 40, 41, 42, 50 (top and bottom), 63 (top), 64 (top and bottom), 70 (bottom), 72 (bottom), 77, back cover (top).

Sandy Welch: 9 (map), 10, 12, 80, 81, 83 (top), 91.

Frances Wood: 1, (upper left), 5, 51, 57 (top), 84, 86 (top).

Copies of the radio programs, "Bayview Live: Stories as Told by our Seniors," as well as tape recorded interviews conducted in preparation for the writing of this book are housed with the South Whidbey Historical Society in Langley, Washington.

Index

A

Ackerman, C. E. 37
Alexander, Mabel 32, 60, 72
American flag 74
American Legion 78-79
Anderson, Andy 79
Azar, Don 85

B

Ballard Boys 76
"Bay View" 31, 95
Bayview Arts 5, 86, 88
Bayview Cemetery 35-36, 95
Bayview Cemetery
    Association 36
Bayview Farm and Garden 4,
    85, 89
Bayview Farmers' Market 3, 89
Bayview Hall 2-3, 5, 59-60, 69
    74-77, 85, 89-90, 96
Bayview Road 2, 34-36, 80,
    86-87, 90
Bayview School 2, 32-34, 60, 69,
    77-79, 85, 90, 95
Bayview School bell 78
Beach Watchers 3
bicycle shop 85
Bill's Feed and Tack 84
Birkenholz, A. F. 48
Bjork, Lisa 79
Blanchet, Father 21
Blankenberg,
    Helen 65
    lumber mill 27
    Paul 27

Brooks Hill Road 57
Bump, George 34
Burk Brothers 29
Burk, John 51
Burk, William 51-52, 57, 96

C

Calista 50
Casey's Market 1-2
Cash Store 2-3, 39-40, 44, 51-55,
    57, 60, 67-72, 77, 80-81, 84,
    86-90, 96
    original Bayview Cash Store
    39, 95, 96
Cherry, Lorna 24
Clatawa 50
Clinton 1-2, 41, 52, 80
Clyde Theater 81
Coffelt, Mary Jane 94
Columbia Beach 60, 63-64, 96
Community Hall, old log 44, 94
composting toilet 5, 88
contra dances 85
Cortes, Jack and Grace 84
Coupeville 2, 22, 40, 55, 57, 95
Cram, Bernie 39-40
Cultus Bay 13

D

Deception Pass 20, 63
Deception Pass Bridge
    2, 80, 96
Digwadsh 13
Diking,
    District #1 47-48, 80
    project 95-96

Doe, Howard 48
Double Bluff 21, 23-25,
    49, 52, 93-95
Douglas fir 1
Dow, William
    and Christine 95

E

Ebey, Isaac 22
Ebey's Prairie 21
Everett 40, 50, 64

F

farming 37, 43
Farrell, Charles 58
ferry,
    Keystone-Port Townsend
        63, 96
    Mukilteo 60, 63-64, 96
    WA State 1
filbert trees 67
Findings Antique Store 84
Finn,
    Catherine 94
    George 94
fish traps 67
fish wheels 67
Flat Rock Productions 87
Fort Nisqually 21
Freeland 2

G

Gabelein, 37, 76
    Alberta 65
    Alvina 65
    Eileen 65
    Emil 48, 69
    Emilie 48, 69
    Eva Mae 75, 78
    Felix 58
    Raymond 48, 65, 74-76, 78
    Raynard 65

Gah-toh-litsa 24
Geoblock 7
German Lutheran church 37
Glencoe 22
Goosefoot Affordable
    Housing Program 88
Goosefoot Community
    Fund 6, 8, 86-89
Goosefoot's Community
    Loan Fund 88
Great Depression 53
Greenbank 2, 87
Greenbank Farm 87
Grimm,
    Fred 71, 94
    Sylvia 94
Grimm's Garage 71

H

Hagglund,
    Herman 65
    Junius 65
Hancock, E. L. 33
Harth, F. A. 36
Help House 73
Henny,
    David 72-74
    Marion 73-74
Highway 525 1, 16, 46, 80-81,
    86, 90
Hofer, Billy 65
Holmes Harbor Rod
    and Gun Club 67, 74
Hunziker, Walter 40

I

Illahee Indians 11
Indian Point 21
Intervale 77
Island County a World Beater 37
Island County Fair 33, 79

Community at the Crossroads: The History of Bayview on Whidbey Island

J

Jensen, Leo 65
Jewett,
    family 58
    Walter (Jack) 23
Johns,
    family 34, 36
    Florence 26, 33
    James 33
    Mary Jane Coffelt 26, 31
    Thomas 26, 31-32, 35, 90, 93-94
    Willie 33
Johnson,
    Jane Newbury 24, 93, 95
    Louisa 24
    Thomas 27
    William T. 23-25, 93-95
Johnston,
    Elizabeth (Betty) Schmidt 56, 67, 69
    Harold 52-54, 56, 58, 67-71, 81, 84, 96
    Judy 56, 71
    Marie Bultman 53-54
    Ray 53, 68-69
    Ronald 53, 68-69, 71
Josephson, John 57

K

Kash Inn 71-72
Kawasaki, Joy 85
Ken's Korner 1
kiosk 6-7
Klallam Indians 11, 13
Kohlwes, 37
    Arlene Alschbauch-Scott 66
    brothers 58
    Clara 66
    farm 50, 66-67
    Frederick 38-39, 58, 66
    Mary 27, 38-39, 46, 65, 76, 94
    Robert 27
    William 27, 36, 38-39, 45-46, 48-49, 58, 65, 76, 94
    Witsoe, Jan 42, 76, 81
Kramer, A. B. 94

L

Lancaster Road 52
Langley 32, 40-42, 50, 52, 60, 68, 70, 72, 77, 79, 81, 95
Langley High School 59, 79
Lanning, Bill Jr. 84-85
loading dock 38
Loganberry Farm 87
logging 29
Lone Lake 2, 8, 15-16, 28-29, 32, 37-38
Lone Lake Mill 28, 51
Lone Lake Resort 51
lumbering 27
Lummi Indians 11
Lutheran Church 72

M

Massey, Howard 68
Maxwelton 41
Maxwelton Beach 13
Maxwelton Road 77
McCloskey, F. F. 94
Meier, Adolph 39
    AKA Meyers, Ernie 39
Melendy,
    C.G. 50
    Carrie Ramstad 53, 70-71, 94
    farm 40
    Frank 58, 70, 94
    J. G. 36
Meyers 37
Millman, R. H. 36

Index

Mitchell, George 40
Model-T Ford 40
Moore, Linda 86
Mukilteo 22, 60, 63
Mutiny Bay 68
Meyers, Ernie 39
    AKA Meier, Adolph 39

N

Newbury, Jane 24, 93, 95
Nisqually Indians 11
Nordhoff, Nancy 86
northern harrier 2
Nourse, Lucille Thompson 59, 65

O

Oak Harbor 2, 53, 60
old growth 76
O'Leary, Mike 68
Oliver,
    Edward 22, 33, 46, 90, 93-95
    Hester 23
    Lake 25
    Melvinia Sooy 23-24, 95
Olsen, 34
    Frank 57
    Mabel 65
Olympic Mountains 1
Olympic Peninsula 10-11, 63

P

Penn Cove 13, 19
Peterson family 33, 58
Phinney, James 94
pile dikes 46, 49
Point Elliott Treaty 22
population 43, 53
Port Ludlow 22, 27
Port Townsend 22, 24-25, 27
post office 40

Protection Island 19
Puget Power 58
Puget Sound 60
Puyallup Indians 11

Q

Queenie 68
Quigley, Roland 65

R

Reed, Jonni 84
roads 40, 71
Rothgeb, Vera 72
Rowley, Maureen and Jim 85
rural character 83, 88

S

San Juan Islands 11
Sandy Point 32
Sanford, Ethel 34
sawmill 28
Scatchet Head 13
School District Clerk's
    Annual Report 32
Schumachers 37
Sears and Roebuck house 87
Seattle 40, 50-51, 60, 64, 75
Sedro 39
Simmonson,
    Dick 65
    Don 65
Skagit Indians 11, 13
Skagit Valley Community
    College 76, 78
smallpox 20
Smilin' Dog Café 4, 84, 86
Snohomish Indians 11, 13, 24
Sooy, Melvinia 23-24, 94-95
South Whidbey School
    District 77
South Whidbey State Park 20

Sudi 84
Sunlight Beach 23, 25, 45-46,
　　48-49, 64-66, 93-94
Sunlight Beach Road 27, 47, 68
Suquamish Indians 11
sustainable building practices 88
sustainable design 5
Swinomish Indians 11

T

Terry, A. A. 49
Thompson, 34
　　Charlotte 65-66
　　Clifford 58
　　Jim 65
　　John 65-66
　　Nourse, Lucille 59, 65
　　Oscar 59, 74
tide gate 48
Tiemeyer,
　　family 37
　　Henry 36
　　Louisa 37
　　William 38, 93
Tscha-kole-chy 11
Tulalip reservation 22

U

Ulrich, Maxine 65
Useless Bay 14, 44-45, 47, 64-65
Useless Bay Golf and
　　Country Club 15, 23

V

Vancouver, George 19-20
Vashon Glacier 9

W

Ware, Robert 94
Watkins,
　　George 94
　　Hazel 71, 94
Webster's Unabridged
　　Dictionary 34
Weedin,
　　family 33-34, 36
　　farm land 39, 73
　　Weedin, Herbert 33, 48,
　　　　57-58, 94
　　Luther 38
　　Susan 45, 48
　　William 35, 45, 48
Wernecke,
　　L. 48
　　Chancy 65
wharf 21, 38, 40, 42, 51
Whidbey Camano Land Trust 87
Whidbey Island Food Co-op 84
Whidbey, Joseph 20
Whidbey Record 54, 73
Whidbey Telephone Company
　　2, 46, 72-74, 89
Whidby Community Hall
　　Association 57, 59, 74, 85
Wilkes, Charles 21
Wood, Enoch 40

Index